Open for Lunch is a deeply moving recollection of difficult lives well lived. Robin Russell Gaiser is a survivor who has overcome personal tragedy and found healing and the ability to reach out to others to share her wisdom and strength. This book holds invaluable lessons for us all about pain, suffering, redemption, forgiveness, healing and love.

—Dr. Lois McMahon, PhD
Adjunct Associate Professor, U. of Maryland

[A]n artfully woven memoir of Gaiser's family and personal landscape as well as her invited encounters with people she didn't know... Throughout the telling of her inward journey are remarkable details that take the reader immediately to "place and circumstance." The stories will also stay with the reader—from start to finish.

—Jan Getz, Peabody Award-winning television producer
former Asst. Professor and Broadcaster in Residence
Point Park University, Pittsburgh

...[A]n amazing story-teller. *Open for Lunch* sings, wails, flails and perseveres with integrity. Thank you, thank you!

—The Rev. Dr. Margaret Ann Faeth (Epis.)

A writer with many stories to tell. (Gaiser) write(s) economically—nothing extraneous to the scene—and with good focus.

—Dr. Rachel Stein, Prof. of English and
Women, Gender and Sexuality Studies, Siena College.

...[A]n incredible, compelling, important piece.

—Dr. Lisa Bloom, Jay Robinson Distinguished Professor
Western Carolina University

Open for Lunch reveals how intuition has guided Robin into loving places, those experiential moments of grace that ring most faithfully true.... A writer ... who chooses to connect rather than ignore.

—Pete Solet, author, *Gliding*
editorial staff, *Sm*

Open for Lunch is much more than the heartwarming stories of Robin's lunchtime encounters with perfect strangers. It is the intimate and unflinching account of her journey to self discovery, release from heartbreak, and the grace that comes from forgiving others and yourself.

—Linda M. Williams, A.B., MEd

Robin Gaiser's prose is vivid and compelling, her descriptions of people and places delicious. You feel like you are sitting there ... and hearing their stories first-hand. It's a rich, eye-opening experience to learn of others' goals, struggles, blessings, and challenges, and how those insights can be applied to your own life's journey.

—Susan H. Wayland, Senior Executive Service (ret.)
U.S. Environmental Protection Agency

Open for Lunch is a heartfelt memoir that examines the profound and lasting effects of the relationship between an only daughter and her mother. Through honest reflection, the author arrives at the difficult truths that have shaped her life—including her penchant for inviting strangers to lunch. These chance encounters unfold in surprising ways, from the mundane to the magical.

—Paula D. Fleming, writer and editor
Former Director, HR Policy and Communications, Xerox Corporation

Robin Gaiser has an extraordinary gift—though sometimes she might call it a heavy burden—for paying attention. She sees, hears, feels and even smells acutely the complexities and contradictions of life—life which plays out as both ordinary and miraculous, ugly and beautiful, cruel and comforting. She writes powerfully of her own experience of being battered by the worst and healed by the best of these extremes. And she also gives us stories of how others have faced these realities, stories that are as varied as the people telling them to her, a stranger who has invited them to join her for lunch. Luckily for them and for us she has learned a thing or two about listening and about coming out whole on the other side of suffering.

—Kit Putnam

I hope that this book reaches the wide audience it deserves. If it finds its way to people who have suffered, they may learn to hope, to seek help, to pray. [It is] powerful, beautiful, unexpected, healing.

—Dr. Carol A. Lisi, Director, ESL Program (ret.)
Alexandria City Public Schools

An honest, courageous and deeply personal story about giving of ourselves and receiving gifts in return. The author helps us to understand the significance of forgiving others and, perhaps more importantly, how to forgive ourselves. In our highly polarized culture that teaches us to be wary of the stranger, she shows us that connecting with "the other" honors our shared humanity and can begin with just a simple suggestion that we share a lunch.

—Connie Curry Hughes, MSW

Pisgah Press was established in 2011 to publish and promote works of quality offering original ideas and insight into the human condition, the realm of knowledge, and the world around us.

Printed in the United States of America

Published by Pisgah Press, LLC
PO Box 9663, Asheville, NC 28815
www.pisgahpress.com

Cover design: Laurie McCarriar, www.artistgeek.com

Library of Congress Cataloging-in-Publication Data
Gaiser, Robin Russell
Open for Lunch
Library of Congress Control Number: 2018959725

ISBN-13: 978-1942016403
Memoir

First Edition
Second Printing
November 2018

Open for Lunch

Robin Russell Gaiser

Table of Contents

PROLOGUE

When I sat down to write *Open for Lunch*, I expected to turn out a collection of short stories about my fourteen years (and counting) of asking strangers to eat lunch with me. My publisher at Pisgah Press and I discussed a host of dining tales, experiences, characters, interactions with my lunch partners. I delivered those stories. But there was more. *Open for Lunch* evolved from a short-story collection into a full-scale memoir.

It happened this way. Fellow writers and my professor Elizabeth Luytens, in four semesters of a Great Smokies Writing Program master prose class at UNC Asheville, began asking keen, probing questions. The first question had to do with Chapter One. "When you write the phrase 'something shifted in me' after you see the face of the woman in line in front of you at Subway and ask her to eat lunch with you, what was that something that shifted?" they asked. I didn't know how to answer.

My classmates pressed on. "Who are you? And what is it about you that invites strangers to eat lunch with you? Why are you doing this?" Again, I didn't know the answer. I assumed asking strangers for lunch was nothing out of the ordinary; anyone could do what I was doing. Simple, just look around for someone who is alone, then ask.

"Oh, no. Not me. I could never do that."

Nearly everyone in class, along with others elsewhere in my life, who heard of my practice responded this way.

I began examining myself in light of these questions, these responses to my lunches, and along came a heart-pounding dive into who, what, why, when, and where. I became the reporter reporting on myself. Soon the stunning stories of my lunch mates took me deeply into my own narrative.

I am a writer whose arms and hands shake when I am uncovering a new or never-told truth about myself or my life. A good reader can tell when an author is withholding information, a fact I learned as a neophyte writer. In my first book, *Musical Morphine: Transforming Pain One Note at a Time* (Pisgah Press: 2016), at first I was afraid to tell all. In my journey from the first memoir to this one, shame, self-doubt, denial, and fear of anticipated reactions from family and friends eventually gave way to much trembling as I told all—at least, all I knew to tell.

As the oldest of four children and the only girl, with a span of fifteen years between me and my youngest brother, what I experienced as a child lived its own uniqueness. My oldest brother and I can reminisce about our similar childhoods, although being a boy in the fifties provided him a mightily different experience in many ways. But my two younger brothers grew up in a household I did not know and do not recognize. Our memories and our individual ways of dealing with them surprise us when we get together and talk about our childhood. Some of my truths have shocked, even displeased them, since they were either too young or as yet unborn when the events occurred.

My relationship with my mother, in particular, was tangled. Counseling nearly all my adult life has assisted me in understanding my enmeshment with my mother along with the unrealistic expectations I carry for myself, learned at her knee. My current counselor, when hearing about my writing of *Open for Lunch*, said, "Well, you know, this is about your mother."

I overreacted. "No! I thought I dealt with that. This isn't about her."

My counselor was right, at least in part. What mother-daughter relationship, the most difficult of all pairings in family life, I think, cannot stand another delving into, another fine-tuning? *Open for Lunch* is by no means all about me and my mother, but my pen hijacked me several times to look around the next corner and see her lurking. In fact, I nearly ran out of ink discovering more about her and my father as well as generations of family, a literal three-way mirror among my lunch mates, myself, and my family. We were so alike; but then, we weren't.

The real names of nearly all my lunch mates have been changed (some even chose their new names) for privacy, as their stories are personal, some never told before. However, Helmer Twoyoungmen (Koskanuba), my dear Stoney Nakota lunch mate, insisted his story be shared without altering any facts. The stories are faithful to what occurred with my lunch mates, and all locations for lunches are true to their actual settings. You might have even spotted me at a local eatery not knowing I was having lunch with a stranger.

It is my hope that this book will provide a feast for you to pick and choose from. When I selected the title with help from my friend Carol Even, I promised myself I would not get too corny with food puns and metaphors. But I can't help myself. So, may you be filled, nourished, satiated from reading *Open for Lunch*. And enriched, fortified, delighted from the full menu of stories and insights I have cooked up. And most of all, may you hunger to learn more of your own story in the restaurant called life.

Robin Russell Gaiser

Asheville, NC
August 14, 2018

Open for Lunch

Dedicated to my husband, Gordon L. Gaiser, my best listener.

Chapter 1

This Faraway Mountain Place

The Walmart wasn't very crowded late this Wednesday morning. I usually chose Wednesdays to shop. On other days I worked part-time at the regional hospital and hospice down the road as a therapeutic musician offering live acoustic bedside music to the critically and chronically ill, the elderly and dying. After observing how my music brought stunning relief to my father as he endured major pain and suffering before he died, I was excited to learn about a training program for Certified Music Practitioners (CMPs). Some of the classes were close enough to drive to for long weekend modules. After two and a half years of study, reading, exams, clinical practicum, and internship, I'd begun this new post-retirement profession.

But every Wednesday, my day off, I'd make the sixteen-mile drive to Walmart, eat a quick lunch at Subway, then go to the grocery store. I had learned to avoid the megastore on Friday evenings when large families from up in the mountains came to town to spend down a wad of cash that had been doled out at the close of the work week. Cheap plastic toys made in China, hunting regalia, sodas, candy, cookies, and snacks filled their baskets along with beer and cartons of cigarettes. Everybody got what they needed for the coming week.

With mixed feelings of agitation and compassion, I noted these habits over and over. *They're wasting their money. What they're eating is unhealthy. They should stop smoking, quit drinking so much soda and beer, save their money*. Then I'd stop—I was being self-righteous, a tendency I didn't like about myself. There had to be more to their stories, and I didn't know them, hadn't lived them.

At least I could avoid the store on Friday nights, but I still felt guilty every time I walked through the doors.

"Mom, don't shop there. It's an evil store. Haven't you read about how badly they treat employees? We never shop there."

"Sorry, but Walmart's the only game in town unless I travel well over an hour on a treacherous mountain road to Saratoga," I retorted, my stock answer to their self-righteousness—so like my own.

Our kids, now grown and gone, lived in cities or sprawling suburban areas, rife with goods and services. They had been reared in the metropolitan Washington, DC area where life unfolded at your fingertips. My husband and I had left six years ago to take on a new lifestyle in upstate New York. We had purchased my parents' retirement home on the shores of the Great Sacandaga Lake outside a small village called Northville in the Adirondack Mountains. Dad was very ill, and he and Mom could not manage the large house and property anymore.

The kids hardly ever visited Northville. I had secretly hoped this new life of ours would attract them for family gatherings, for holidays and vacations, that my roots and my favorite place for these events would become theirs. Northville was a place where, as a child, I had felt safe, loved, connected. But the lake, pool, boats, water skis, picnics, ice cream every night, campfires on the beach, were not the big draw for my children as they had always been for me. I pictured a future with grandchildren zipping down the waxed sliding board of our pristine pool, wobbling on water skis as they pulled up behind our speedboat on the lake. I imagined telling stories together after dinner in the Adirondack room of our house, walking with them on the country road searching for animal tracks or scat. But clearly that was not to be: yet another source of a growing unrest about living in rural upstate New York.

My shopping list was short, and I knew the Walmart layout well, so I shopped quickly, checked out, and wheeled my cart over to the Subway. The yellow and green wall, bright booths, large posters showing fresh vegetables, and the clear, clean curved glass cover over the sandwich fare was a welcome relief from the dark March day. I felt my mood brighten. Even lunch at a Subway was a treat in this faraway mountain place.

A woman stood in line ahead of me. Her lavender-gray hair, thinning so that her beige scalp peeked through unkempt curls, made her look old. She wore no hat or boots. Her glasses were dated, yellowed plastic frames with bifocal lenses, the little half-moons in the glass visible when I peered through them from behind her. Her jacket was a simple quilted maroon car coat, and she wore mint-green polyester slacks. Her shoes were somewhat worn down white tie-up sneakers. I could not see her socks.

My analytical inclinations actively engaged as they always did when I was drawn to someone new. *Who is she? Where does she live? Is she from these parts? What's she doing in here today? Is she alone?* We both moved down the line ordering our sandwiches. She dug into her overflowing black handbag and pulled out cash to pay for her food, then turned with her tray. I saw her face for the first time.

That's when something shifted in me and I spoke to her. I didn't understand why it happened.

"Um, I'm by myself and it looks like you are too. Would you like to eat lunch together?" I surprised myself with these words. Would she reject my offer? Think I was crazy, pushy? Was she really by herself or would someone join her? We stood there face to face for what seemed like a long time. She looked me over, then spoke. “I think that would be okay. Where do you want to sit?”

“How about that booth over there?” I said, pointing to a small curved wooden booth with a yellow Formica tabletop.

She walked over to the booth while I paid for my lunch, then I joined her, sliding sideways on the bench to sit, placing my tray across from hers on the table top. My awkwardness pushed me to speak first. “Thanks for accepting my offer,” I said looking across the small shared space between us. “I don’t know what prompted me to ask you except we were both alone. I thought it would be more enjoyable to eat lunch with someone.”

“That’s fine with me. Wednesday is my day off. I do the shopping and eat lunch out.”

I asked her where she worked.

“I don’t work. I take care of my husband. He’s not good,” she said looking down. “He’s got diabetes real bad and just lost all the toes on both feet. He can’t walk no more.” She looked back at me and I saw tears running down her cheeks. She poked around in her purse for a Kleenex and wiped her face. “I didn’t mean to cry in front of you,” she said.

“I think you have plenty to cry about. Tears help sometimes.” I waited, then asked if she had anyone assisting her with his care.

“Just my sister. She’s the one taking care of him today so I can get out. But she’s not good either. I’m waiting to pick up all his drugs at the pharmacy. I do that on my day off, too.”

She was worn: sad eyes, tired wrinkles, stooped shoulders. She unbuttoned her coat, revealing a pink sweatshirt painted with playful pastel kittens chasing balls of yarn.

“My grandmother had a shirt like yours. Do you have a cat?” I said trying to get to know her, take her away from a very ill husband and a life of constant care for him.

She brightened. "I have three cats. Want to see pictures of them?"

I wasn't a cat lover, but I of course I said yes. She had already begun to rustle in her handbag for her wallet. While I unwrapped my sandwich and opened my bag of chips, she fingered through a pack of rubber-banded photos and credit cards thick as a deck of playing cards. She pulled out several photos and laid them across the table in a line. She pointed, "This is my kitty; he's a little devil. I just got him after Boots died. Boots was seventeen."

I raised my eyebrows. "What's his name?

She laughed. "Bad Boy."

I smiled and told her we had a cat like that when our first son was barely a year old. Not a good idea. After too many scratches on the baby and too much climbing up the inside of our new drapes, we found the kitty a new home.

She pointed to the other pictures. "This is Lily; she ate my daylilies when we first got her. She's my cuddler." Pointing to the last picture she said, "And this other one is Jack. He's my husband's cat. Climbs up on his lap all the time now that he's in his recliner, sleeping most of the day."

"You know, you told me your cats' names but we haven't even shared our own names. I'm Robin."

"I'm Lois. Nice to meet you, Robin." I started to reach across the table to shake hands but decided only to acknowledge her with a quick nod of my head. I had noticed that women up here did not shake hands with each other the way they did in the DC area.

"Do you live nearby?" I asked.

She said she had lived on the Mountain Road all her life. I began to formulate a bigger picture of her and her family.

"I live outside of Northville, on the lake," I said. "Been there for six years. My dad's family's from the Village. Do you know any of the Russells?"

"I think I heard of one or two Russells. One was a music teacher or something." I told her that the music teacher was my Aunt Helen and that my cousin was the nurse at the central school.

"I've heard of your cousin, but her last name's not Russell, is it? The grandkids go to Northville Central. I think my daughter called her a couple times when they got real sick. Your cousin's a nice person."

"My cousin is Lynne Russell Barnett. She seems to be everybody's nurse." I paused then continued. "So, you got grandchildren," I said. She pawed through some more of her photos and presented me with a school picture of a boy about ten or eleven.

"This one's my oldest. Named Walter after my husband, but we call him Pudge. He's always been a little on the chubby side. He was a big baby. Near ten pounds. My daughter had to have a section to get him out."

"Big boy, very handsome, too," I said. She stared at Pudge's photo for a long time, grinning at her first grandchild. "I nearly raised all of them since their parents have to work all the time. I'd still have the two little ones, the girls, except Walter got so sick. He's all I can manage." She pulled out another picture of a plump toddler with big blue eyes and curly blond hair pulled back with pink plastic kitten barrettes. "This one's named after me." She beamed, then looked over at me. "You got any kids and grandkids?" she asked.

"Three kids, one married, but no babies yet. They all live far away. I miss them a lot, but they have new careers, work hard. One's finishing up another college degree."

"I don't know what I'd do if my kids lived away. We're all on the Mountain Road. One big happy family. Here's the other kids. Four girls and another boy," she said laying the photos across the table in front of me. Sharing the six photos of her grandchildren and the three photos of her cats felt like she had opened her hope chest to me.

She finally got to eating her sandwich, a three-inch version of my six-inch sub. No chips. No drink, except water. I wondered if money was an issue or if she was just a light eater. I knew folks on the Mountain Road struggled to make ends meet. She was of medium build and ate slowly, deliberately. Maybe she was prolonging her time away from her ongoing duties at home.

I began to study her more closely. She might not have been much older than I was, but I assumed her life had aged her. Her hair needed a good cut and color, her clothing was faded from many washings and of a style more fitting to a much older woman. I remembered her white tie-up sneakers and lightweight coat, not much protection from the vicious Adirondack winters.

When she finished her sandwich, she looked at her watch. "Oh, I guess I can pick up Walter's medicine now. And I just talked your ear off. But I really enjoyed eating lunch with you. I'm glad you asked me."

"Me too. A real pleasure, Lois. You have a beautiful gang of grandchildren and I love your cats. Let's hope your husband improves. Along with this nasty weather."

"Yes," she said again looking down. I reached across the table and lightly patted her forearm. I regretted my comment about her husband getting better; diabetes was not a curable disease. She gathered her sandwich papers and food tray, slid out of the booth and stood up.

"Nice meeting you," she said buttoning her coat with one hand. She did not linger, but hustled over to deliver her trash to the collection bin. I watched her as she disappeared into the aisle leading to the pharmacy.

She had already stepped back into her role as wife and caregiver, but I hoped our time together might have brought her more respite than just a couple of hours out of the house.

I sat still in our booth, sipping the last drops of my Coke. I wondered if she knew she had filled up a lonely place in me, that she had stayed a gray dismal day in my life with her willingness to have lunch with me. I hoped I would run into her again on her "day off."

March in the Adirondack Mountains is mucky. It always amused me when the weather forecasters nonchalantly mentioned "possible snow showers" for the day. Snow showers up north translated to rapid accumulations of one to four inches. An accumulation like that in Northern Virginia closed schools, clogged the beltway, stranded commuters, and lined grocery stores with anxious shoppers stocking up on toilet paper, milk, and beer.

Today on my drive here the sky had fallen apart, dropping large wet snowflakes on the windshield as I steered my Passat wagon along the windy two-lane highway, Route 30. It was sixteen miles along the only main road between our house outside Northville, population one thousand, and the next larger town, Gloversville. There was no intermittent sun trying to warm the earth in between the "snow showers," and the road easily accepted the slushy mess. One to four inches, I thought.

My back seat always held extra gloves, hat, scarf, and boots, and I was already bundled against the damp cold, the most offensive of winter's relentless six-month blast. Discovering Cudd'l Duds, sleek soft long underwear which snuggled my legs beneath my jeans, was one of my first northern winter shopping triumphs. As a relative newcomer my "blood was still thin," my cousin Lynne said, laughing when she learned I donned my extra layer of warmth early in October. If she layered for winter, the outdoor thermometer read minus degrees. She had lived in Northville all her life.

Her personal thermometer exuded warmth in all seasons. She had been like a "nurse on call" for my father as his life inched away, and again when I dealt with emergencies with my elderly mother.

Lynne became my confessor and ally as I entered into the mysteries of end-of-life care and my father's death, just three months after our arrival. Her father, my dad's younger brother, had died shortly before our move to the Adirondacks. She was accustomed to answering her phone around the clock, patiently responding to desperate parents or other residents of the Village inquiring about illnesses and injuries.

Many of her callers lived, like Lois, on the Mountain Road across the bridge over the lake, just outside of town. The mountain people, as they were called, barely scratched out a living in this rural location, often relying on government assistance to feed and clothe their families, and heat their makeshift dwellings. Extended families clustered together on property where ancestors had staked claims decades before. Cousin Lynne knew them all.

Though larger than Northville, Gloversville was a gray, dismal city, its dilapidation a painful reminder that the heyday of fine leather goods production had migrated to China. I turned the Passat left at the only stoplight en route to the grocery store. Besides the endless mounded snowbanks along the main highway, the parking lot held piles of filthy snow, melting and then re-freezing with every charcoal layer of road dirt, snowplow scrapings and chemicals accumulated since October's first snowfall. The slush splashed the sides of my car as I pulled into an open spot.

As always, I picked my way through the parking lot, careful to avoid stepping into the minefield of new potholes and to sidestep patches of possible black ice. You had to pay attention to survive this lifestyle.

For some reason I was fixated on getting fresh cilantro in the produce section. Maybe I was yearning for the vast selections of herbs and vegetables in Northern Virginia, the choices of so many nearby stores ready to fulfill your every whim. More likely I was still trying to make living in this rural, lonesome climate work for me, a game in which the presence of one particular herb would make it all okay. It had been my idea to move to the Adirondacks to get away from the craziness, the traffic, the hordes of people in Metro DC. A quiet lake house near my extended family's ancestral home, the only real roots I had, had been a long-held dream of mine. Now I had it, but the dream was beginning to unravel.

With a full grocery cart, minus cilantro, I trod lightly across the parking lot to my car and loaded my bags into the trunk. I had set myself up for disappointment with desires such as fresh cilantro in Gloversville in what, to me, ought not to be winter. Even hoping to meet someone I knew at the grocery store or Walmart and asking if they wanted to join me for lunch was, perhaps, a way to sabotage my dream. And yet ... I had met someone for lunch after all.

As I backed out of my parking spot I glanced over at Walmart and wondered if Lois was already home tending her husband, ready to receive her grandkids when the school bus chugged up the icy Mountain Road, and petting her precious cats. The heavy sky blended with the outdated gray and blue siding of the aging Walmart, another shabby reminder that this area had been neglected, forgotten. I made the right turn out of the parking lot and headed north to my home on the lake.

Despite regular Wednesday trips to Walmart and the grocery, I never saw Lois again.

That worried me.

Chapter 2

Determined to Win

Not ironically, my first urge to ask strangers for lunch coincided with my early years of work as a Certified Music Practitioner. Working one on one, bedside or chair-side with long-term and terminally ill patients, awakened me further to the pain and suffering in this world. In a sense, I began to think we were all in need of care. I saw families and friends along with staff benefit from my music as much as the patients. And I know the music ministered to me as well. Music has always soothed, moved, inspired me.

Dr. Oliver Sacks, the noted neurologist and author, says it so well in his last book, *Giving*, completed, literally, on his deathbed. He writes, "I have come to think of almost everyone with whom I come into contact as a patient in the emergency room. I see a lot of gaping wounds and dazed expressions."

I think that Sacks's "gaping wounds and dazed expressions" are symptoms of a pervasive isolation and loneliness in our society, possibly quite simply, the human condition, since at heart we truly cannot know each other. We are lost. We are hungry. Social media, reality shows, talk shows, anonymous phone calls masquerade as real human contact. We no longer live with extended family. Doctors and other clinicians lack compassion, exhibit little or no "bedside manner" when we are at our most vulnerable. Death and grieving astound us. Marianne Moore states it succinctly when she writes, "The world is an orphan home."

When I examined the faces of the supposedly well and well-off, those countenances often held the same look of desperation as the faces of my ill, elderly and dying patients. I readily picked up on their moods, their feelings, their illnesses. Could asking a stranger to eat lunch with me open the same kind of healing opportunity as offering music to the ill and dying?

In the rooms of hospices, hospitals, nursing homes, private homes, I concentrated on easing the pain, the fear, and suffering of my patients, but it was no accident that visitors, families, medical staff, administrators and housekeepers lingered in the music, telling me later how it released tension, brought necessary tears as they eavesdropped on the sounds floating down the hallways and into their offices; how the music elicited their stories. I began to notice that when the music really connected with my patients, I felt whole, joyful, worthwhile. Although not intentionally, I became a beneficiary of my own reaching out.

Even though I wore the face of a put-together, satisfied person, one of the "well and well-off," I experienced my own inner turmoil, my own dark and stormy past, and now a churning present as I realized that living in the Adirondacks, fulfilling my long-held dream, was not working for me anymore. I was an orphan in this place.

My face, my actions did not reflect what I felt inside. I had learned to smile, buck up through the worst of circumstances in my life: young widowhood, cancer before I was forty, severe anxiety morphing into panic disorder and agoraphobia, consequent prescription-drug addiction and rehab, near death from errors during a hysterectomy for a pre-cancerous uterus, two serious car accidents with subsequent back and neck surgery, broken bones from osteoporosis, two more cancer scares. What roles did these play in my reaching out to others, either to those obviously in pain or those I sensed were struggling with life behind the scenes, as I was?

I am the oldest of four, and the only girl, born to young star-gazed parents who fell in love as teenagers and then were separated by World War II. When my war-hero father returned home to his family in Niagara Falls, New York as a decorated USMC bomber pilot in the Philippines, he and my mother married immediately. I was conceived on their honeymoon. Not the plan. I was born nine months and two weeks later to the day, a fact my mother repeatedly emphasized. All too soon, I replaced her as the beautiful darling girl in my father's life. While Dad insisted Mom not disturb him when he studied his college engineering problems at his desk, I was eagerly welcomed into his study when he heard me awaken from a nap or toddle down the hallway outside his door. I felt my mother's resentment toward me all my life.

During the War while my father was away, my mother, a statuesque, blue-eyed blonde, completed her college degree in voice and piano at West Chester State College. After their marriage she began teaching music in the school system in Niagara Falls, NY, where she and my dad moved in with his parents and younger sisters to save money. Dad was attending the University of Buffalo on the GI Bill and working two part-time jobs. As a young couple they enjoyed the luxury of dancing to the Big Bands at Dad's fraternity parties or going to the movies while my grandparents and teenage aunts babysat me. The whole family attended the large brick Baptist church where Mom sang alongside my grandfather in the adult choir. Dad, a singer himself, could not spare the time for choir.

My mother's childhood had been a mishmash of moving from place to place, shuffling from one relative to the next; her story was full of unanswered questions and surprises, which she deigned to share with me only later in my life. Although she enjoyed privilege, it came at a huge cost to her. My father's large, inclusive, demonstrative family, overflowing with hugs and kisses, provided the stability and affection my mother found lacking from her early life and from her limited number of taciturn relatives. She herself was a chilly, unemotional person, a narcissistic woman who made me a slave to her neediness, her desire for status. I was so tuned to her, I struggled to know myself. She controlled and criticized my every move, my body, my choices.

And especially my music.

She didn't know what to do with me when she began giving me piano lessons at age five. I had been picking out tunes on the piano for two years, so she started me off in an advanced piano book which required playing with both hands together, not one at a time, like the beginner books. Even so, when she played my lesson songs for me, I could play them right back with my little girl fingers on the piano keys. "Look at the music, not your hands," she instructed.

"But see, I can play the music myself, mama."

"That's not the right way." Her lessons with me continued with the same method for the first few weeks. She'd play, I'd play back watching my hands find the notes. Exasperated, she wrote "LOOK AT THE MUSIC!!!!!" in big red capital letters at the top of the music page. I had to ask her what she had written, since I was not yet a reader.

When I did not, or perhaps could not comply with her rules, she stopped giving me lessons. That didn't deter me from playing the piano, but as I taught myself, my way, she'd march into the living room and stand behind my back watching me. "Your fingering is terrible, do it this way," she'd say pushing me aside on the piano bench so she could demonstrate proper fingering techniques. "That's an A sharp," she'd yell from anywhere in the house. Soon I learned to wait until she left the house to play to my heart's delight, no music on the music stand. And when I was eight I begged to learn the violin, an instrument she knew nothing about. My private teacher taught me to read music, but also delighted in my other musical gifts, incorporating them into my lessons. I especially enjoyed playing violin duets with him, sometimes making up my own harmonies.

When I was seven or eight, my mother sat me down at the square game table in our living room, eager to teach me the fine points of chess, checkers, bridge, her secret weapons for success. And then she would bask in beating me soundly, analyzing the stupidity of my moves as my anxiety and shame mounted. There was only one board game I enjoyed with her, Scrabble. My cleverness with words outshone her strategies with game pieces, playing cards. I refused to join her in her games, but she continued to engage in Scrabble with me, concentrating hard to defeat me at my game. We played Scrabble up until her dying day; she was determined to win. But I held my own.

My father on the other hand was playful and funny. He was dashingly handsome and very personable. Everybody loved him. He told me I could become anything I wanted to be. He joined neighborhood games of badminton, baseball, hide and seek. When it snowed he spun me and the other kids around on our sleds which he hooked with ropes to the back of his VW; he took us ice skating and played crack the whip. He taught us folk songs when we traveled in the car, bought our family a boat and taught us to water ski, a sport he loved himself. His childhood had been somewhat idyllic, except when World War I took his father away and Dad became the man of the house at fourteen: he worked at the local movie theater until midnight, sold papers and magazines door to door to pay the rent and feed and clothe his mother and siblings, paid his older sister's college tuition, all the while attending the high school for the gifted.

He was creative and clever, and I think the war and the times ruined his opportunity to know his heart well enough to follow a suitable path in the arts or humanities. Engineering and flying jets in the Marine Corps as a reservist may not have been the best fit for him. Although he loved the thrill and the risk of flying and made the rank of full colonel in his forties, I sensed his underlying depression and anxiety, feared his temper. I tried my best to please him, to be the perfect child, avoid his anger. Mom told me he ground his teeth while he slept, called out, turned fitfully in bed. I heard him belittle her at home and in public; despite my efforts he enacted harsh discipline on me and my brothers, erupted into angry outbursts, and used alcohol and cigarettes to numb his pain. With the latter, he ruined his health.

However, to the outside world Dad appeared to be the happiest guy around. He knew names and stories, remembered a library of jokes, volunteered in the community, the church, the Masons, the Scouts. He was absent from his family, but present for others.

Both my parents were demanding of themselves and others around them, including me and my siblings. They overcommitted, overworked, overachieved. Since most of their activities involved being away from home, as the oldest and a girl, I was handed adult responsibilities; as early as six years old I was tasked with babysitting my brother. Since my other brothers were spaced far apart, there always seemed to be a fussy baby or a wide awake pre-schooler, a table full of dirty dishes or a stack of ironing taking me away from my free time, my friends, my homework, or my bedtime. These duties, plus expectations of exceptional achievement in school, music, church, Girl Scouts, became my norm. As a grade-schooler I bit my fingernails, had difficulty sleeping, developed stomach trouble.

But we were "The Russell Family," dressed up, idealized, smiling for the cameras.

When I look back at my extended family's history, I find a line-up of high achievers, hard workers. Even my female ancestors attended college or normal school. For those who did not go on for higher education, there was never a lack of skill or work ethic, allowing for advancement in their careers and respect from their communities. Music flowed freely on all sides of my family, especially church music, since church attendance and strict adherence to biblical teaching dominated family life on every front.

My mother's parents, Halsey and Helen Lewis, both held degrees, he in business and economics from Boston University, she in nursing from Lankenau Hospital School of Nursing in Philadelphia. Hidden from his parents, they dated and married in Boston, had my mother, then vanished from Halsey's upper-class family who lived near Boston on six rolling acres in a sprawling yellow and white mansion. When my mother first told me how he disappeared with his young family to Virginia to assume a job as a college professor, she did not address why, so I surmised that Halsey wished to break ties with, possibly rebel against, his snobby, prejudiced, wealthy parents. They ended up in Newport News, VA, where Helen, my infant mother's mother, contracted tuberculosis and was sent to a sanitarium for treatment; as a result, my mother was cared for by a live-in black nanny. And shortly after their move, her father Halsey died suddenly, precipitating disruptive changes in my mother's life, including more moving and new caretakers.

I know only that Helen was from a poor family and orphaned at an early age, then cared for by an older sister, Ethel, who treated her badly her entire life. Helen enjoyed a close relationship with her other sister, Edythe, until age and infirmity separated them. I remember going with my mother to visit both of them when they were in their eighties in West Chester, PA, a duty my mother took seriously. Helen was a closed-mouthed, distant grandmother to me, although she loved being in the midst of our busy family when she visited.

Halsey's parents, Cora and Ashton Lewis, were highly educated, cultured people. Cora, a poet, graduated from Mount Holyoke with a degree in literature, Ashton from Boston Conservatory with a violin performance degree. Cora was the daughter of real estate tycoons in New Jersey, and both she and Ashton invested in the real estate market in Boston near their home in Gardner, MA, my mother's birthplace. Ashton concertized, composed and conducted the orchestra that later became the Boston Pops. Cash flow from their properties afforded travel, lavish entertaining, and finery. They adhered to strict New England-style manners and looked down their noses at persons of lesser social, economic or educational standing, especially blacks and immigrants.

My father's parents, Walter and Esther Russell, felt more like parents to me than grandparents, since we lived with them until I was four when Dad, newly graduated with his engineering degree from University of Buffalo, took a job necessitating a move to the Philadelphia suburbs. Grandma Esther was a natural at mothering me—kind, soft, competent, loving. She knew somehow that I was a highly sensitive child, prone to upper respiratory illnesses and tummy aches; she also recognized I needed quiet and darkness to sleep, that I cried when I became over-stimulated, and I liked having down time, time by myself to explore, create, assert my independence. She included me when she cooked, sewed, washed and ironed, gardened or rode the bus to appointments. She was never too busy to read a story or rock me in her arms, take me out to feed the squirrels, push me in the swing my Grampa Walter built for me. During World War I, while my then-teenaged grandfather served as a Navy radioman, she earned her teaching degree at Pottsdam Normal School in upstate NY, and then taught until he returned and they were married. They were both from Northville, which to this day remains as the extended family's touchstone. Grampa Walter held no formal degrees, but he was a genius when it came to electronics, succeeding in his careers and maintaining a ham radio presence until he died. He sang tenor in the Baptist church choir, often performing solos on special occasions. I was their first grandchild and adored them as much as they adored me.

Esther's parents, Charlie and Nora Duncan, well-respected, well-known as Northville residents, maintained roots all the way back to the Mayflower. Charlie did woodworking, carpentry, painting, wallpapering, and construction and served as the Village fire chief. He and my father were close. Nora, who came from a prosperous family outside of Northville, was a homemaker with four children, a large garden, and several chickens. Both were known for their generosity to the community and church. The extended Duncan family had established and built the Northville Presbyterian Church, where my parents and Gordon and I became members after our move to Northville for retirement.

Carrie and Maurice Russell, my grandfather Walter's parents, met at the Northville Baptist Church where he was the new young minister from Union College and she was the church organist and choir director. Preacher Maurice died of stomach cancer when my grandfather was four; Carrie and my young grandfather then moved back into her family's spacious, well-appointed home on Main Street. Her father owned a strip of prosperous businesses within walking distance from their home.

Samuel, preacher Maurice's father, was from upstate NY, but uprooted his wife and large family to become a fiery circuit-riding Baptist preacher circulating in the rural South. Samuel's long absences caused his wife to move with the children, including Walter, back to upstate New York to be near her family. Samuel eventually joined them.

Themes of church, music, wealth, status, family, accomplishment, independence, community service, outreach, education and conservative religious belief and practice dominate the landscape of my past. On the surface, they may not set me apart from themes running through other extended families.

But as I absorbed the stories of my random lunch partners, I heard unique, distinct, stunning differences among us mixed with the often uncanny commonalities. Every aspect of their stories informed me, aroused me, blessed me; and through them I delved more deeply into my own story.

Chapter 3

Unsettling

That mucky March day in the Adirondacks, after eating lunch with Lois at the Subway and hearing her story, partially filled an emptiness I felt as I shuttled alone around the grocery store and the Walmart, lost in my thoughts, silently owning up to my own loneliness, my sadness, the toll life in the Adirondacks was taking on me. I am certain my inner dialogue that day prompted me to risk that first move to ask a stranger to sit and eat lunch with me. Maybe it was my own pain and suffering, usually unspoken, that caused me to recognize, sense the struggles of others at a deep, visceral level.

My husband, Gordon, and I stayed put in the Adirondacks for a couple more years as I devoted my energies to my work as a music practitioner. That work, although deeply satisfying, was intense and draining, so I usually drove straight home, needing to withdraw and regenerate rather than reach out and look for more ways to extend myself. I joined a group of local women for lunch on Fridays. I hoped to assuage my loneliness, become part of the in-crowd, learn the latest Village scoop. But often this gathering exacerbated my feelings of not belonging there. As Northville natives, they talked about people and events that were foreign to me. I just sat there trying to fit in while they chatted away. Instead of having fun and feeling connected, I often felt invisible, even more lonely. How could people be so non-inclusive? Didn't they want me there?

The long winters and the rural lifestyle prompted me, more than Gordon, to rethink our retirement to the north. He had been reared on a farm in north-central Iowa and always found voluntary moving a curiosity, not a necessity. He was used to long frigid winters and loved a blizzard with a couple of days of howling winds, severe temperatures, and blinding snow. Weather like this frightened me, especially when our power went out. Unlike me, he had lived in the same house all his life, a white farmhouse on a gravel road, miles from town. I had been uprooted multiple times to live in various suburbs of large cities. As a result, I was the one who shopped for houses and urged our moves. My mind had already begun wandering off to possible relocation spots. I felt we had given and gotten plenty from our eight years in Northville, and it was time to make a change.

I understood Gordon's lack of enthusiasm, especially about moving from this idyllic spread on the lake. He loved our 1898 two-story red barn housing his father's antique John Deere tractor that we had had trucked to our place from Iowa. Over a two-year period Gordon had meticulously restored it in the spacious, musty barn. When he debuted it in the Northville 4th of July parade, folks along the parade route hooted and clapped to see him atop his pride and joy. He loved maneuvering his meaty Husqvarna mower around the two and a half grassy acres of our property, the lake breezes erasing gas fumes and any concerns he harbored.

Each summer he harvested colanders full of fat blueberries from our bushes down by the lake. One year he picked so many, we had to buy a small freezer to store them, even after sharing with neighbors, family and friends. He made pies and pancakes all year long with the blueberry bounty. He loved his inherited barnful of my father's old equipment. He had revived the leaf blower, snow blower, chain saw, and edger while my father was still living, delighting both of them with a machine concert one evening as the smoky old relics coughed their songs into brisk, late-summer air. He enjoyed the camaraderie of the men at our church, some of them old Adirondackers, who gathered at their own table spinning yarns, chewing the fat each week after the service during coffee hour.

He did admit he wanted more intellectual stimulation, closer amenities. I was worried he would become one of the old, tired men sitting around the church coffee-hour table. He was highly educated, well-read and well-travelled, unlike his comrades. He loved art and history. I didn't want those sides of him to go untended—he probably would have let them go (save travel) since this atmosphere was familiar to him from his childhood. After foreign travel, or while he was actively engaged in an educational endeavor or working on a project, he and I enjoyed spirited conversation. I felt our marriage depended on it.

An opportunity for me to present on the topic of healing music at a national conference in Nashville, TN, prompted a car trip south for us. I had heard about Asheville, NC and its beautiful environs as well as its rich heritage of music and crafts, but we had never ventured there. We agreed to stop there on the way back from the conference. After a successful presentation and an all-expenses-paid stay in a fancy hotel in Nashville, we loaded ourselves and my instruments into the car and drove to Asheville. The temperate climate, the arts, nearby college classes, excellent medical care, along with more mountains beckoned us to return. Even Gordon was enticed.

Meanwhile back in the Adirondacks we told no one of our thoughts about moving on. A small town like Northville would not take kindly to losing us. We secretly made another short trip to Asheville and began looking at housing arrangements with a realtor. We decided to return and stay in Asheville for the month of March, mucky old March, that transitional time of year. This would be a test. Would it be like the Adirondacks in March? We arrived in Asheville during a snowstorm on March 1st and hardly made it up the mountain road to the little log cabin we had rented for the month. My spirits sank, thinking Asheville was already failing the test.

We unloaded the car in the snow, cranked up the fireplace in the log cabin and went to bed. The next morning a bright sun and pristine blue sky greeted us along with a line of yellow daffodils, already poking their heads up, outside the cabin window. I felt hope. The snow had actually begun melting overnight and it was gone by noon. This was a good sign!

Our real estate agent had already set up a number of house tours for us on the third day after our arrival. Seeing spacious homes on large tracts of land that required mowing and tending gradually morphed into a more realistic look into making this move. Gordon at first resisted communities where much of the outdoor work was included for a monthly fee. However, he frequently traveled and often our yard, which he normally cared for, would grow two feet high with grass and weeds during his absence. Even he complained about mowing then. We finally agreed that a home off Beaverdam Road in a community up the side of a mountain was exactly what would work for us. And in a week, to our amazement, our offer to buy it was accepted.

We discussed keeping the lake house in the Adirondacks, but maintaining an 1863 farmhouse required vigilance and care; managing it long-distance was not a sensible option. We laughingly called it "this old house" after the TV show by that name. Gordon always had something to fix: the ancient artesian well water system, the leaky kitchen window, our rural mailbox repeatedly knocked over by the snowplow; or wild critters to manage: mice, red squirrels, chipmunks, bats. I always felt the latest disaster would upend us, but he thrived on the excitement.

He would miss these handyman opportunities, but not if we still owned the big spread and lived far away. Even when we traveled for a few weeks in the winter the house and property became a worry, a liability. We hired professionals to rake snow off the roof, plow our long lane, and check for leaks in the roof from ice build-up. We poured antifreeze in the toilet bowls and left faucets dripping to ward off broken pipes. Living up there was a challenge.

I knew I would I miss the Adirondack summers, the smell of pine trees mixed with fresh pure mountain lake water; the sound of tree frogs singing in unison at dusk. I would miss sliding my kayak easily off our beach and paddling out to the water lilies floating next to the small island where eagles nested. I would miss the sound of the water lapping at the side of my boat, the drone of hundreds of bees dipping and retreating from the pink lily florettes as I sat, motionless, watching for eagle activity. I would miss the tiny summer lake church where I sang and played music for services and eventually took over my mother's position as music director when she decided to move to a warmer climate and a continuing care residence community in Norfolk, Va.

I would miss the camaraderie of Ladies of the Lake, my gang of adventurous women who assembled every Tuesday year-round for outdoor sports apropiate to the season: snowshoeing and cross country skiing in the winter, hiking in the spring and fall, kayaking and swimming in warmer weather. As a founder and organizer of this group, I did not feel lonely or left out since most of the women were only weekend or summer people who didn't launch into discussions about Northville history or residents I didn't know.

Despite these regrets, we sold the house on the lake and moved to our new mountain home in western North Carolina. With less maintenance, less concern for traveling, a ready community of fellow transplants in our new neighborhood, temperate seasons, arts, education, convenient medical care, and outdoor activities, life opened up again, became less difficult. I could even walk to a year-round pool for exercise for my ailing back and jostled nerves. I had begun to realize how important regular exercise was to thwarting my age-old battles with insomnia and anxiety.

I recall the last person I approached with a request to eat lunch with me before we left the Adirondacks. While I waited to be seated at House of Pizza, a young man dressed in a well-tailored suit, crisp dress shirt and matching tie pushed in through the double doors of the restaurant and joined me in line to be seated. His attire caught my attention: it was not the dress code for Gloversville, NY. Up to this point I had never asked a strange man to join me for lunch.

"You're all dressed up today," I said as an opener. "If you're solo, would you like to have lunch together?"

He readily agreed and the hostess seated us in a cozy booth by one of the only windows in the dark dining room.

"I work across the street at Ruby and Quiri," he answered. "We have to dress for work." I knew the furniture and appliance store well. Gordon and I had bought several items there. The store was the best in town. Or should I say it was the only one in town. I acknowledged his statement with a nod.

He seemed distracted, nervous, fidgety. I hoped he had not felt obligated to accept my invitation and now regretted his decision. When the waitress approached our table to take our orders, he lingered over the menu before deciding what he wanted for lunch. His hesitancy to order surprised me; I assumed he dined here often and would know exactly what he wanted since his workplace was close by. Finally, he ordered exactly what I had: house salad and one slice of cheese pizza. Water to drink.

He handed his menu to the waitress and spoke immediately. "I'm getting married in two weeks. But I'm not sure I'm ready," he said wide-eyed, looking as if he wanted a response from me.

"That's a hard place to be. Is there any way to postpone the wedding?"

"No, not this late. All the invitations are out; the church, the flowers, the food are all set. I just came from my final tux fitting. We were supposed to get married next year but my fiancée's father got cancer and the family wants to make sure he sees his only daughter get married."

I shook my head side to side then spoke. "Sorry about her father. So, your fiancée is the only girl," I said gently. "So am I."

His eyes lit up and he smiled broadly as the conversation turned to his intended.

"She's special. We met at the community college. She's a nurse. Here, you want to see a picture of her?" He turned his phone sideways to face me, then scrolled along the screen and stopped at a picture of a tall, young, striking dark-haired woman in a sundress.

"She's beautiful. It looks like she's at the beach."

"Yeah. I took Alli to the Bahamas and proposed on the beach at sunset. I had the ring in my pocket. She was so surprised she cried for probably an hour afterward." He glowed as he elaborated on his story; how he kept the secret from her, but not their families. How he knew what ring she would choose and what ring size she wore.

"I can tell how special she is to you. You should see your face right now." He blushed.

"I do love her. Maybe I just have regular getting-married nerves. I hope so. I want our marriage to work. I don't want to lose her."

"My husband was so nervous at our wedding that he sweated right through his suit and developed a visible large oval of perspiration on the back of his jacket. Everyone ribbed him about it. We've been married for 39 years." I could see him relax.

As we finished our lunches he told me he thought he would be okay with the wedding. "I think I just needed to tell someone I was worried."

"Thanks for telling me. You seem a lot better since you talked about it."

He rose, left a cash tip on the table. "I need to get back to work. I'm on commission. If I'm not there selling, I don't make any money."

I got up and followed him to the cashier to pay for my lunch. When he completed his transaction he turned to me. "Thanks again for listening. I'm going to be fine."

"My pleasure. I'll be thinking of you and Alli on your big day." We shook hands and he pushed his way back out of the double doors of the restaurant. I signed my credit card slip, thanked the hostess and left. I could see my young friend crossing the street to Ruby and Quiri.

I never learned his name or saw him again, but I enjoyed my role as his confessor. Maybe my work as a counselor had taught me that active listening often was the greatest gift a person could give to another human being. I sat for a while marveling how he just opened up to me, pondering what had drawn me to him in the first place.

Chapter 4

The Nicest Thing

My artistic, creative juices began to flow again in our new Asheville environment. Gordon eagerly signed up for multiple classes at the university, dove into renovations of our new home, and walked the gorgeous mountain trails in our neighborhood every day. We enjoyed new friends, joined a progressive church, and delighted in the vibes of downtown Asheville. Many, like us, were not locals: unlike Northville, in fact, most of us were transplants.

Volunteering as a therapeutic musician at a nearby nursing and rehabilitation facility took the place of driving long distances and working a regular schedule. I preferred the freedom to offer healing music when the spirit moved me. As usual, the music was embraced, worked its miracles in the rooms of patients in this large, rather impersonal building. I had hoped there would be differences between rural upstate NY and western North Carolina, but it was not so. The antiseptic smells, the crying out, the desperate faces, the blaring TVs matched the environment of the extended care facility where I had worked in Gloversville. My eyes opened even wider to the deficits in our care for the unwell, the elderly and the dying.

After our move to Asheville I continued seeking out solo diners to eat lunch with me. If loneliness drove me to do so, I was not aware of it. My ongoing belief that we all harbor loneliness to some degree and that we deserve to tell our stories, along with my love of sensitivity to those around me more likely moved me to continue my practice of asking strangers to dine with me in restaurants around Asheville. And as usual, I was alone when I did so.

But on one occasion I wasn't.

Gordon was with me when I noticed a young, round, somewhat unkempt young woman join us in line on a Sunday at Subway on Merrimon Avenue. She was the only other customer in the restaurant besides us. She wasn't dirty, except for her fingers and hands, covered with something black, her finger nails tainted with the same dark stains. At first I mistook a smudge across her left eye as an injury, and was secretly afraid she may have been a victim of abuse. But with further inspection, the apparent black eye looked more like she had wiped her brow with the back of one of her sooty hands.

Leaning in close to my husband so she couldn't hear me, I half-whispered, "Hon, I want to buy that woman's lunch and ask her to eat with us." He frowned, hesitated. I saw a familiar stiffening of his shoulders. "I'm not comfortable doing that," he said, and turned to order his sandwich. I surprised myself with the idea of not only dining with her, but purchasing her lunch. Where had that notion come from?

I moved closer to him. "I was really uncomfortable when I did this for the first time," I said, and let it go. Pushing my idea on him didn't seem right. After decades of marriage, I knew trying to talk him into things wasn't a tactic that worked. And if I chided him into situations, I ended up feeling responsible for how things turned out, guilty and apologetic if they turned out badly for him. I began to rehearse my idea and felt uncomfortable myself. What if asking to pay for the lunch of a stranger could come across as an insult, an insinuation that I thought the person could not afford to pay for herself. What was I thinking?

He and I ordered our sandwiches and moved along the counter toward the cash register. As he reached for his wallet, he turned to me and said in a low voice, "Ask her if she wants a drink and chips with her sandwich." I blinked in disbelief, as if to ask if he really meant it. I knew he did. He is a man who doesn't commit to such an uncommon behavior if he isn't sure he wants to participate.

I took a few steps back to the woman and quietly spoke to her, being careful not to overwhelm, insult or embarrass her. "My husband and I want to buy your lunch today. We just feel like we would like to treat someone and here you are next to us in line." She stopped in her tracks, her mouth fell open, she lowered her head and began weeping. When she caught her breath, she raised her head and spoke, "No one has ever been this nice to me before."

I didn't want to believe her. Surely, a stranger paying forward for a sub sandwich had to be low on the list of generous gestures. But I guess it wasn't so for her. I added, "We hope you can join us to eat."

"I would like to do that but I've been up since midnight and I need to take a shower and get to bed. I'll be back up at midnight tonight."

"What work requires that schedule?"

"I deliver *The Asheville Citizen Times*. Next week I'll be on the job for a year," she said, standing taller as she spoke.

"I hope you get a raise," I said smiling. She looked sideways, then back at me. "Don't I wish. I make $380 a week now. I'll get $400. And they'll still give me the back roads: gravel, rocks, potholes, mud so my car gets all beat up. I already need new tires."

"Do they pay for that?"

"No, they don't even pay for the plastic bags we stuff the newspapers in. On rainy days we have to double bag. And Sunday, we have to buy the big bags to stuff in all the ads."

I shook my head.

"I have to live at home. I'm trying to save so me and my boyfriend can get our own place."

By then her sandwich was wrapped and paid for. She had declined chips and a drink so she was ready to go. "I'll never forget this," she said, beginning to tear up again.

An awkward moment passed between us, a time saturated with clues about how to say goodbye. I made the first move, inching forward with my head and shoulders. She also moved forward and at the same time we extended our arms and embraced, her sub sandwich in its crackly bag dangling from her hand.

"Thank you," she said, wiping her cheek and creating another black smudge across her face.

"You're very welcome. Thank you for telling me about your work. I'm going to tip our newspaper carrier a lot more. Enjoy your lunch, and get in a good nap."

She smiled, and pushed open the exit door to walk to her car, a beaten-up, mud-crusted small black SUV. At that moment I felt like I should have offered her more than lunch and a dining invitation. Again my eyes opened to the truth of another human being's struggle. The appearance of our paper, neatly bagged and delivered on time while we slept, now held more meaning for me, another opportunity to appreciate rather than expect.

Perhaps the story of the newspaper carrier could have ended when Gordon, after his initial discomfort, asked if she wanted chips and a drink with her sandwich. This felt more like his story, not mine, not hers. Something had changed in him. But my reaction to his reluctance was also different. I held back, felt a new easiness with the fact that my thing did not have to be his thing.

Whatever made him shrug his discomfort with inviting and paying for lunch for a stranger was not my doing. As we ate our lunch together, I didn't launch into discussing what happened. Gordon is not one who appreciates being gushed over; he likes to mull things over in his own time, then, perhaps, talk about them.

I kept the incident to myself until later, on the way home in the car, I spoke. "I had no idea newspaper carriers are so badly paid and that they're the ones buying the plastic bags, bagging the papers, and paying for repairs on their cars."

"Yeah," he said. "Not good."

I let a little time pass and added, "Have you noticed on really wet days the paper is double bagged?"

"Yeah."

Short answers from him are typical, and often a sign he is not ready to talk. The rest of the way home the only sound was the whine of the car engine as we wound up Beaverdam Road. Gordon could not see the satisfied smile spreading across my face as I began to cherish what had just transpired between us and the newspaper carrier at the Subway.

Chapter 5

Golden Living

It wasn't lunch time. Hurrying up the grassy hill to the sprawling red brick facility, I hoped I would catch patients still awake after their noon meal. Oversize glass picture windows shot blinding reflections in my eyes as the sun leaned toward the mountains behind me to the west. The uninspired, rectangular building with its perfectly spaced square windows and aluminum-roofed portico entry reminded me of motels along Route 1, where my family stopped overnight on marathon car trips when I was a child in the '50s.

Even on overcast days curtains at this facility were drawn across the windows, leaving patients' rooms rather dismal and depressing. I knew from experience that a dark room was not always a sign that a patient was napping. Frankly, patients slept on and off twenty-four seven. A lone voice often queried me about whether it was day or night when I entered these rooms. And daylight interfered with nonstop television, flickering and blaring fake company into their rooms, whether they wanted it or not.

I had been volunteering at Golden Living for a few months now. The cheery, upbeat sign at the entry of the bumpy macadam driveway leading to the parking lot elicited my sarcastic back talk every time I read it, since life there was neither about living nor was it golden. After our move from the Adirondacks I chose this nursing/rehab facility along the main road for its proximity to our new home. Inquiries at the local hospice facility, where I would have preferred to volunteer, although farther away, indicated there were plenty of services in place, including therapeutic musicians. Golden Living boasted no such amenities.

As anticipated, the Golden Living staff was hungry for any free service for its residents. My offer of therapeutic music was embraced and welcomed by the recreation director with whom I communicated and to whom I reported. Over time I envisioned making myself and my music services so indispensable that I'd slide right into a part-time paid position there. I was a credentialed professional and deserved payment for my work, but complementary healthcare was not always recognized or rewarded for its value.

By contrast I pictured Harbors Edge, my mother's tony retirement highrise on the water in Norfolk, Virginia, with its fancy entry, its elegant dining room, its spacious ballroom. Nearly every time I visited her, she arranged for me to give a special music program to her cohorts (for pay) and after delivering more than an hour's worth of music in the ballroom, she hauled me around to entertain, soothe, wake up folks in memory care, assisted living and nursing care. I never said no to her, my ongoing pattern of pleasing her, even though I was annoyed and so exhausted after all that giving I could hardly sit up for dinner in the formal dining room. After such intense music-making I could not sleep as I relived the experiences, saw the faces I had interacted with that day. I knew Mom's insistence on my music was about showing me off, putting me on her accomplishments list. I admit I drank in the appreciation from the staff and residents, but I felt uncomfortable since the music I offered was not intended to showcase me.

Today, at Golden Living, I strapped my standard nylon string Goya guitar, my favorite accompaniment for my singing, and my light-weight, honey-toned Irish lap harp to my back; then clutched a low-pitched Native American Flute, snuggled down in its colorful bag in my hand, and tucked two small silver harmonicas into my pocket. This array of varied musical equipment covered most of the patent conditions I usually encountered.

Patient conditions, if I even knew them, and their reactions to the music dictated what kind of music I provided: instrument choice, style of music, tempo, key, mode. Lyrics or no lyrics to songs also made a difference. With fragile or actively dying patients lyrics—along with steady beats and recognizable melodies—were eliminated, to assist a person's passage from this world to the next. For pain or anxiety, a steady beat might work, but then a floating rhythm could do the trick as well. Since I offered live one-on-one bedside acoustic music and played without a music stand or iPad blocking my view, I was able to set up my portable chair very near my charges and observe them closely for the tiniest responses to the music. Even a tick under the chin or a restless hand or foot gave me information.

My knowledge and intuition for choosing the right music had become the talk of the nursing floors at former places of employment, and now it caught the attention of the staff at Golden Living. Often nurses, aides, even support and office staff showed up, silent and still, leaning against the door frames of the rooms where I played and sang, mesmerized by the music's magical effect on the patients. I am sure they came to take in the music for themselves as well. Their jobs in this place were not easy. "Your music comes over this building like a balm," a social worker told me.

Loaded with my musical freight, I huffed up the final incline of the hill, walked across the circular driveway under the portico to the double-wide glass doors. With my free hand I buzzed myself in. No ambulances or other transports were lined up outside the doors, not even a family vehicle loading or unloading a wobbly, weary passenger blocked the driveway. Maybe a quiet day at the nursing home.

Hand sanitizer in a white plastic box hung on the wall just inside the entry doors and, after setting down my instruments, I pumped the clear, alcohol-laden gel on my hands. I took this precaution both before and after my sessions with patients, a universal standard taught in my therapeutic music classes. The strong scent of hand cleaner often overrode unwelcome odors present in healthcare facilities. This one was no different. Today, someone nearby badly needed a shower. Because I was especially sensitive to strong smells, becoming desensitized to the inevitable odors of nursing homes and rehabs had challenged me when I first began the work. This aspect of being a music practitioner had not been covered in classes.

As usual a group of droopy-eyed patients, strapped in wheelchairs, staring into space or snoozing with their heads down, met me in the entry foyer. Light streamed in the front doors and I wondered if these patients asked to sit there day in and day out to see daylight. A man's eyes looked through me and followed my steps as I turned left down one of the long hallways to the recreation office. The so-called office was a mere corner in the group room where I stored my coat, uncased my instruments, and hung my official badges around my neck on a green cord with a silver clip.

I was a volunteer here, but I behaved as a paid professional. When I initially presented myself to the recreation director I handed her a packet with my updated résumé, reference letters and therapeutic musician credentials. She raised her eyebrows, took a step back. "You didn't need to do this, but I'll keep it on file." Like so many, she really did not understand what a Certified Music Practitioner did. She assumed I'd be the typical "He's Got the Whole World in His Hands" musician strumming away to a group of patients in the facility's dining room. Of course,

I could and did do that, but my specialty was reaching those patients who weren't able, or who were unwilling, to attend group events—the terribly underserved in this world of nursing home care, the ones sunk into hospital beds, trapped in the tiny world of their overstuffed rooms, moored to machines humming and spitting day and night.

Once I assembled myself and my instruments, my policy was to locate a floor nurse and ask if any patients had special needs that day. With four hallways and seventy-seven beds, mostly filled, choices had to be made. There were often requests for music for the lonely and the depressed ones, those on hospice care dying slowly in the silence and darkness of their rooms, those who had restless anxiety or chronic pain.

Luckily, I caught the attention of the charge nurse before she scooted off in her usual flurry to answer the incessant buzzing of call bells. My personal plan for my days at Golden Living always included sweet Violet, whether her name was mentioned by the nurse or not. And I saved her for last.

The nurse pointed to a room down the east corridor. "He's just lost his wife, last night. She was his rock." Off she flew after that one comment, so I proceeded to his room, not knowing how he might respond to my offer of music.

He lay in bed in a heap of unruly covers. His head, resting on a pillow, was turned toward the door. His room was darkened by the same drawn curtains as all the other rooms at Golden Living, but a small bedside lamp illuminated his face enough for me to see he was red-eyed, his graying hair uncombed. I spotted his lunch on a tray table, pushed away and uneaten. He didn't move his head when I entered, but he lowered his eyes to examine my guitar.

I spoke softly. "The nurse sent me to you. Music might help you get through the day. She told me about your wife." I waited. He inhaled, exhaled, raised his head and mumbled a half-hearted "Okay," then lay his head back down. "If this is not good for you or if you've had enough, please tell me." I opened my portable chair and sat down next to his bed, first situating my guitar on my lap, then up against my chest. I had left my other instruments out on the hall for now. Who knew what music would suit him? Grief, like depression, was a hard one. You could either play into the sadness, even coax out emotional response, or attempt to lift it, distract the patient with upbeat music, recognizable tunes and lyrics in major keys, lively rhythms.

I began playing my guitar, classical style, slow tempo, improvising long phrases of arpeggios from major to minor chords and watching his expression. If the minor chords evoked too much emotion I would stick with major chords. He silently wept through both styles of music as I expected he might. I continued for a few minutes and eased into a stopping place and looked at him, raising my eyebrows as if to ask, "More?" He motioned with his head for me to go on. I added improvisational humming to the guitar. He relaxed his facial muscles and lowered his shoulders. He surprised me when he spoke during a musical pause. "Can I tell you about my wife?"

I stopped the music, laid my guitar flat across my lap and leaned in toward him. As I looked more closely into his face I saw his mouth ease into a gentle smile, his weary eyes twinkle though his tears. For nearly an hour, he spoke tenderly about their fifty-two year marriage, their kids and grandkids, their travels together. He cried intermittently and reached for my hand.

So often I witnessed music lift spirits, open pathways to memory, allow patients to tell their stories. My distraught patient telling the story of his beloved was moving him into the important business of grieving and healing well. A new strength was seeping into him. When he shimmied himself up to a sitting position, squared his shoulders, and held his head erectly, I knew the music had done its job for the moment.

He made a request for me to push his tray table over so he could inspect his neglected lunch. When I sang and played my parting song, he cried and smiled at the same time. *Let me call you sweetheart, I'm in love with you.*

I folded up my chair, told him I would check in on him another day, then said good-bye and walked toward the door. When I glanced back toward him to say another good-bye from the hallway, I thought I saw him eating.

The energy drain from intense sessions such as this one leaves me depleted, often eager to get things over with and go home, but I am keenly aware of the numbers of patients who benefit from music. Golden Living has no lounge area where I can sit for a while, catch my breath, eat a snack, process my own emotions. And so I push myself to continue, room after room, song after song, ignoring my own needs for those of others, as I was taught to do.

I stopped midway down the hall at the water fountain, slurped voraciously from the steady stream of cold water and stood up. Right then, I decided to give into myself, cheat, end my day early after a trip to the other hallway to see Violet.

Violet was usually mentioned as a candidate for music by the nursing staff, so I wasn't really cheating. She had recently become bedridden and therefore missed the camaraderie of group activities; she slept a lot, picked at her food, had lost too much weight, and was understandably sad, lonely. I saw it in her eyes. But to me, she was a breath of fresh air.

I walked around to her room and tapped on her door, which was partially closed. "C'mon in," I heard from behind the door. Laden with instruments and my chair, I pushed the heavy door open with my shoulder. Violet's head flew around, her face lit up. "It's you, it's you."

She had visitors, two young persons standing on the window-side of her bed. "Kids, this is Robin. She makes me so happy with her music. Isn't she beautiful? Look at that smile? Her skin. Her eyes. Her hair. I just love her." I was used to this gush of compliments from Violet, welcomed them, even sought them out, but I had never received them in the presence of others. I felt my face flush.

It was also Violet's custom to rave about my voice. "Rich and soothing," she'd say, then go on to marvel about all the instruments I played. "You make me so happy. I just love you. I've never heard any music like this."

Who wouldn't want to be in the presence of all this love and admiration? No wonder I saved Violet for last after I made the rounds to other less effusive, sometimes grumpy or non-responsive patients. She lifted my spirits, praised my music, my looks; offered me recognition, validation. I knew I welcomed, wanted, even craved her attention.

I'm embarrassed, even ashamed to acknowledge that I possess this shadow side of my very giving self, a self that will cross over too many times to a place where I am the one in need when I am supposed to be the one giving. Violet easily filled my emptiness, gave me joy, said the words I longed to hear all my life. She made me smile, feel good about myself. But I often left her after our sessions, wondering whether she gave me more than I gave her. At Golden Living I had volunteered as a giver, not a taker.

The equation of giving in my life had always tipped in the direction of my being the giver. Even the over-giver. Both parents demanded much of me, and the church of my youth pounded in the notion of giving more than receiving, tending your neighbor not just as yourself, but more than yourself. I think of my Grandma Esther, my Aunts Nan, Ruth, and Marg giving all they had to family and church. Closer to home, my mother's life revolved around her volunteer jobs as the music director at every church she and my father ever joined.

As a child I longed to be part of a family that relaxed together during Christmas or Thanksgiving or Easter holidays, but my mother's overcommitment to church music with choirs, soloists, instrumentalists for religious services, multiplied in number during these times of year in the church; and I was included in all of it as a musician. After these events my mother would fall in the door, don an apron, and put a festive dinner on the table for the family.

Did she enjoy any of it? I knew to mind my business and do what I was told during these seasons. She flew off the handle easily, complained about how tired she was, and shot out resentment to anyone who did not share her burdens. All of us kids were targets for her anger. But not my father. She didn't dare. Along with a demanding job, he was overcommitted to the church as well, and his short fuse went off on us kids. And my mother.

Give, give, give became my mantra as well, easily learned from frantic overcommitted parents. Add to this that my mother's needs and demands strangled me into being her caregiver. Not yet a teenager, I behaved like an adult in our house, the one who not only meticulously tended to brothers and household chores, but also the one tasked with the job of figuring out what would please my mother. She only knew she lacked something. It was my responsibility to fill that emptiness. She was not warm and loving, appreciative, or praise-giving, and I could never satisfy her. As I took stabs at pleasing her, tried harder and harder, she criticized my looks, my outgoing personality, my dreams, my music.

My artistic talent in music, art, and writing gave me serenity and joy as well as recognition; but not from home. I did receive glowing compliments and appreciation, my name in the newspaper, a monetary reward for poetry, kind words after a musical solo, which felt really good to a kid starved for love. However, after performances, prizes and exhaustion, I was tutored at home about how to do better the next time so I could be perfect, given lessons about how I had to use my talents, lest I lose them. Both mandates were God's edict for all of us. With those messages, of course I sought outside pats on my back, praise for performances, and continued to give and give, fearful of parental disapproval and God's grim warning.

So here's my sweet Violet. Her words, her recognition tumbled out of her every time I showed up to give her music. She filled me up. Yes, she derived major benefit from my presence. She ate her lunch, even cleaned her plate when I offered her music. Her depression lifted and her face glowed as more oxygen entered her lungs when she sang along to songs she loved. And I think she felt special and loved, the way I did when we were together. Maybe, the giving and getting equation balanced out in the end.

I stood inside her door like the pied piper, still red-faced from her welcome. Who were these visiting "kids" as she called them? They were all chewing something. I saw the huge cardboard pizza box spread across the blankets on Violet's lap as she lay in bed. The pizza had to be freshly-delivered since the scent of steaming, yeasty dough made me swoon. This sure beat the pasty, overcooked meals from Golden Living's kitchen. Sometimes the smells and sights of their cafeteria food made me nauseated.

"You've got company and you're enjoying lunch. I'll circle back later," I said turning to leave Violet's room.

"No, no, stay right here," she commanded me through a mouthful of pizza.

I remained standing in the doorway, undecided about whether to stay or not, eyeing the twenty-something duo. The young man's dark hair was short, well-trimmed, tousled loosely on top, like the college kids on the street; he wore a chocolate brown leather jacket over a pastel polo shirt. The girl wore a nubby, pink sweater that looked hand-knit, her shoulder-length brown hair shining in the light of the window. A silver necklace fell just to the first button of her crisp white blouse. Fingernails, visible on the hand that held her slice of pizza, were well-manicured, polished with a subdued rose color.

"Hi," I said, moving into the room and next to Violet's bed. "Violet called you 'kids?' Are you children, grandchildren, friends of this wonderful woman?"

"Great-niece and great-nephew," said the young man. He had the same forthright, but loving manner as his great aunt.

"Do you want some music while you dine?" I smiled. Offering music to patients while they ate meals or snacks, took medicine, even had blood drawn, was a common practice. I enjoyed many memories of full plates emptied, thick liquids consumed, as well as pills swallowed easily and blood taken freely from a tiny shriveled arm while I filled the rooms of patients with music.

"No, no. We want you to eat lunch with us. There's too much here for just us," Violet said pushing the pizza box across her lap, closer to me.

I hesitated. Accepting food from a patient, sharing a meal with her family seemed like tipping the "give" barometer too far in the "get" direction for me. I answered that I couldn't accept their offer. Violet gave me a stern, insistent look. "You're like family to me. So eat."

Reluctantly I propped my guitar against the side of the bed, set the other instruments by the door. "Okay, one piece." I knew I was hungry, weak after the earlier music session with the grieving man, and frankly the pizza was tempting. I took a slice and enjoyed every morsel. I even took a second piece at the urging of the nephew. After everyone had their fill, nearly a third of the large pizza still rested in the brown box.

"Do you live nearby?" asked the nephew as he bent over Violet's bed to fold in the lid of the pizza box.

"A mile away," I said, curious about why he had asked that question.

"We have to drive to Greensboro, so why don't you take the rest of the pizza home for dinner."

Now the "get" button was really being challenged. "Couldn't you eat it along the way?"

"No, no. You take it," Violet chimed in. "Now let's have some music." I guessed that was the way it would be, but I still felt uncomfortable. She was giving me too much.

I wiped my hands on a napkin and took up my guitar. There was no chair nearby so I raised my leg and set my foot on the stainless steel rail underneath Violet's mechanical bed. Then I rested the guitar body on my raised leg and began a musical introduction. I wondered what music would span the age gap between the kids and their aunt. I came back to behaving like a professional therapeutic musician with my decision that the music session belonged to Violet, not her guests.

You are my sunshine, my only sunshine, you make me happy when skies are gray. To my delight the kids joined in and all four of us livened up Violet's room, and possibly her hallway with our spirited voices. Hardly skipping a beat, we sang Beatles songs, folk songs, gospels, hymns, laughing and inventing lyrics when we didn't know the words.

Violet sang and clapped, jiggled her body, waved her arms in time to the music. The pizza box, dancing with her, nearly slid off her lap. Her niece caught it just in time. Occasionally the thought of who was giving to whom sneaked into my head, but my joy in the moment silenced that voice.

I saw her great-nephew turn his wrist to read his watch. "Yikes, it's been an hour," he said. "We've got to get going." His sister agreed with a nod.

"Aunt Violet, this was so much fun. I love you," he said bending over her bed to kiss her squarely on the lips. I saw her take his hand and caress it for a long while after he stood up. Her blue eyes moistened.

"Aunt Vi, I'll get back over to see you during spring break," the young niece said squeezing her way past her brother to lean down and kiss her aunt.

"You bet you will. And we'll have pizza and invite Robin to come, too."

The kids and I started to shake hands when they were leaving, but spontaneously we hugged, a warm trio. My guitar, still up close to me, almost made a quartet. I asked again if they didn't think they should take that pizza with them, but they edged out the door, blowing kisses to Aunt Vi as she wildly sent air kisses back to them.

"Aren't they the best?" she asked immediately after they disappeared.

"They are. I think it's because they have the best great-aunt in the world."

She lowered her eyes. "Their mother died when they were teenagers and I had them come live with me."

"I can tell you're very close. A lot of love for each other." She raised her eyes and I saw they were beginning to droop. She laid her head back on her pillow and accepted my offer to lower the upper part of her bed and sing one of her favorite songs before I left. She took a deep breath and sighed.

Hush-a-bye, don't you cry, go to sleep ye little baby. When you wake, you shall have, all the pretty little horses.

By the time I sang the last two lines, her lips were parted slightly, her eyes fully closed; and her chest was rising slowly and rhythmically beneath her blankets. She didn't move when I slid the big pizza box off her lap and snuck out of her room to lay it on a nearby bench outside her door. I crept back in and collected my guitar and other instruments and stood by her bed a moment to watch her sleep.

A new lunch story had just unfolded: I was the one invited to enjoy lunch with strangers. Not my usual. But we were hardly strangers for long. Sweet Violet's hospitality, her open heart for her niece and nephew, and for me, her infectious love, drew us together, erased reluctance we may have felt. Of course, sharing fresh pizza and laughing and singing together weren't bad ways to bring strangers together, either.

I eased out of her room.

This dear woman. A mother to me.

Chapter 6

Bastard

Unlike Violet, I didn't want my mother sitting there. The swimming pool was my sanctuary; my rhythmic breathing and stroking lap after lap a spiritual recharge, a reprieve. I had gone to the pool to escape her scrutiny. I am an expert swimmer, so her attendance may have meant she wanted to enjoy the ease and beauty of my body gliding through the warm turquoise water of the indoor pool. I wanted to think so, but as I swam and she sat there observing me, the softness of the water, the loveliness of the moment chilled to loathing her presence. I dreaded the completion of my lap swimming, knowing I would emerge from the water fully exposed, standing nearly naked next to her in my clingy bathing suit. I could already hear her words. "Oh, you've put on some weight–your thighs, your midsection," she'd say, her eyes scanning me up and down.

After Gordon and I made the long drive from Asheville to Norfolk, she would greet us in the lobby of swanky Harbors Edge, where she lived as an independent resident in a tony, spacious, two-bedroom condo on the seventh floor. With a stiff hug and hurried peck on the cheek, she would step back and look me over from head to toe. Gordon, like my brothers, was immune from this inspection ritual.

So I stood there dripping wet in front of her in my bathing suit, ashamed of my body but seething, holding back the angry responses on the tip of my tongue. This was my mother's lifelong ritual with me. She criticized. I took it in.

For life, we sat on opposite sides of the aisle, especially when it came to music-making. She, the classically trained pianist and vocalist, looked down on my ability to play by ear, compose, improvise, memorize. I did learn to read music when I was allowed to take violin lessons (after promising I would obey my violin teacher's instructions). But I used musical scores as "suggestions," the mere mention of it causing her to frown, squirm. I was not seen as a real musician in her eyes.

I found playing in orchestras, executing solos and duets, singing in choirs and ensembles exhilarating. Over time I taught myself to play multiple instruments, joined bands, composed, arranged, recorded. In college I gave guitar lessons in exchange for having my English papers typed, and while my children were young, I opened my own music business where I offered guitar and dulcimer lessons in a home studio Gordon and I built together.

My approach to teaching incorporated every learning style, capitalizing on the inborn tendencies of the students who walked thorough my doors. I could easily tune in to their learning styles, their levels of comfort. For visual learners I chose music books for them to follow and wrote down every lesson detail. For the auditory ones, I recorded their lessons so they could listen at home and we spent most of our time together playing songs over and over, music propped on the stand for lyrics, as "suggestions." For kinesthetic learners I instructed the students to feel the frets on the fingerboard for guidance, to move their bodies to rhythms, to tap their feet. Missed notes were an opportunity not a mistake. Weeks with little at-home practice opened the door for creativity with what we had to work with, not admonishment for lack of preparation. When I look back at that period of lesson-giving, I remember the wide range of age and ability of my students. And especially touching are the memories of the parents who placed their children with disabilities in my care for music lessons. Somehow I just "knew" how to teach them.

Meanwhile my mother continued to give piano lessons in her living room, still wedded to her theory notebooks and classical teaching style. Her open criticism of my music making had changed to a more skeptical opinion, but I still felt a sense of inferiority when she observed me playing or singing. She made it known that she knew about music and I didn't. She had the music degree.

When she sat in the audience during my performances, my attention often wandered to her face. I suppose I was still looking for a smile, a sense of approval. She scowled when she listened, her eyes stared ahead, never connecting with mine, unlike the rest of the audience, and her body remained rigid, motionless in her seat. Was she just enduring my music? I learned to avoid looking at her, even asked her if she knew she appeared to be unhappy during my performances. She denied she was. But I always braced myself for criticism. "Robin, isn't that supposed to be in the key of G? You played it in E."

I didn't want her sitting in the audience. Her presence made me work too hard. I had to accept that the only sign of her approval of my music was a collection of my CDs spread out on her coffee table. Bragging rights in front of her friends.

My body, my music. And my hair, my shoes, my clothing, were all fair game for her cruel remarks. "Robin, those shoes make your feet look big." Or "I like your hair this way," she would say pointing to a picture of me from earlier years that she often laid on her kitchen counter for me to see. "That sweater pronounces the size of your hips," when I modeled a new purchase. This notion of my being "too big" bled into criticism of my personality. "You're too loud and bossy," she'd say. I came to understand this later in life as my natural leadership abilities. In that way I was like my dad, but girls and women to my mother were not supposed to take the lead.

She shopped at Lord & Taylor despite her insistence our family never had any money to spare. A big treat was for her to take me to lunch at the Bird Cage restaurant upstairs in the Lord & Taylor nearby. First, I'd follow her around from department to department and watch her try on elegant, stylish clothing in the dressing rooms, often acting as her attendant fetching different sizes and colors for her. After a full morning of that we'd go to lunch. I was all done up in a fancy dress and uncomfortable shoes she insisted I wear; we'd sit in the fussy, formal lunchroom and eat tea sandwiches and salad together, her choice for me from the limited menu. After lunch I accompanied her to the shoe department where she pored over shoes and accessories to match the new outfit she had purchased in the morning. It only occurred to me later in life that on these shopping trips she never bought me a thing, except a lunch I didn't care for.

As I began taking writing classes in Asheville, I shared my early short vignettes and stories, essays, poetry, and finally chapters from my first book with her. "When am I ever going to see this book finished?" she asked repeatedly. I knew she wanted more coffee table bragging rights.

"Did you read the three chapters I sent you?"

"Yes. Chapter eighteen's too long."

One time, seated across from her at the round table in my den after eating a lunch and defeating her at Scrabble, she settled back in her chair and began telling me a story. I was recuperating from surgery and had taken a chance to invite her to keep me company, always hoping that our time together might bring us close, might help me understand this critical, insensitive woman.

"Did I ever tell you the story of my birthday?" she asked. I shook my head no, and leaned in across the Scrabble board, closer to her. Her face hardened, her eyes looked beyond me out the window to the woods behind our house before she shifted them back to me. "I didn't know my birthday was in April until I was eighteen. It was always celebrated later, in September."

She went on to tell me her mother, a non-driver, insisted my mother get a driver's license. They took the bus to the DMV together and when her mother filled out the necessary paperwork, my mother saw her birthday clearly written under DOB as April 7, 1924. She pointed to the date, shaking her head, questioning this apparent mistake. Her mother's stern facial expression and dismissive wave of her hand toward my mother silenced any discussion. The issue was never brought up again.

My mother teared up. "I was an illegitimate child."

And so part of the mystery of her parents' disappearance from the Boston area away from the scrutiny of Halsey's aristocratic, cultured, snobby, ultra-religious family and their friends, was revealed in her birthday story. That afternoon, as we sat in silence across the table from one another, I saw that my mother's face still wore the shame of her beginnings. I was forty-two when she finally told me.

I still marveled at her previous stories about her father's family knowing nothing about his marriage, his daughter, his whereabouts or his job until he died suddenly from peritonitis. When my widowed grandmother, still suffering from tuberculosis, knocked on his family's ornate front door in Boston with my mother, then four years old, in tow, they were not ready to accept these in-laws, strangers bearing fitful news. In a short time, however, despite their shock and grief, they took a fancy to my mother—their unexpected granddaughter—and took them in, even hospitalizing my grandmother nearby so my mother could stay in touch with her.

This arrangement lasted ten more years. The wealthy Boston grandparents embraced my mother and raised her in their large well-appointed home; she was privileged with music lessons, proper schooling, expensive clothing, extensive travel, and the company of persons with impeccable manners and superb educations. She was taken to church every Sunday and schooled in fundamental Bible study. Her grandmother, the graduate of Mt. Holyoke and a religious woman as well as a poet, and her grandfather, the concert violinist, conductor and composer, did everything in their power to ensure my mother turned out well, upheld their reputation, carried on the family legacy of culture and education. But I doubt they knew her true birthday.

What was missing in my mother's upbringing was interaction with other children, especially boys, the normal rough-and-tumble, a family life with parents, siblings. The family's hired help tended household chores, laundry, yard work. She was told she was exceptional, special, kept away from the less fortunate, the less than. Prejudice against immigrants and blacks crept in to this echelon of society and a sense of superiority reigned in the house. Yet my mother's grandparents loved her fiercely and insisted she stay in contact with her ailing mother, a task my mother despised.

When she was fourteen, her mother, now cured of TB, whisked her away from the Boston family and the privileges of that lifestyle to West Chester, PA, where they moved in with the financially strapped, mean Aunt Ethel, her husband and five cousins in a large house with boarders living on the third floor. My grandmother worked long hours to maintain my mother's Boston lifestyle, which aroused jealousy from the cousins and nasty criticism from the aunt. They called her "Queen Bess." My mother hated her mother for forcing these circumstances on her and maintained that anger toward her for the rest of her life.

And so, despite certain hardships, my mother was showered with attention and privilege; she was kept in the spotlight, the center of attention with her Boston family as well as her own mother. She continued to enjoy an outpouring of resources for lessons, schooling, travel, and clothing from both families even though her mother often could not afford it. She was not required to work as her cousins did, and was unused to dirtying her hands doing household duties until she lived in Pennsylvania. She had never interacted with young children as a baby sitter and had not even held an infant in her arms until I was born.

I did not feel safe with her as my mother. I craved tenderness, sensitivity like the kind my Grandma Esther gave me, but my mother was clueless, helpless as a parent. I don't ever remember sitting on her lap and reading a story with her. I only recall sitting with her on the piano bench while she sang children's songs—but mostly popular tunes—while she played. Her needs precluded mine. And she was bound and determined she would control me, mold me into the girl, the woman she decided I should be. I tried to please her, be the daughter she desired, but I never succeeded.

From an early age I disliked her and vowed not to be like her. I climbed trees, played in the woods, shot baskets with the boys, had a million friends. There would be no degree in music, no fussy clothing, no snobbery. I would be the best mother, the best wife, the best teacher. I would not criticize. I would be welcoming, open. I would reach out, befriend, invite all people, with no regard to color or status. I would love. I would be kind.

Ironic. In my lifelong pursuit to not be like my mother, I placed similar impossible standards on myself and flogged myself when I could not maintain them. My own mantra for perfection nearly killed me. Physical illness, emotional breakdown, low self-esteem, the need to please doomed me until I began to dismantle the damage through intense counseling.

My mother was one of the most difficult patients I encountered when I offered her music during her final illness and death. I could not seem to reach her. That same scowl, those same fixed eyes and rigid body didn't respond to the music I sang and played for her. I had hoped that as I sat by her side during her last days, I might experience something beautiful: our coming together, her finally saying out loud that she loved me, that I was a wonderful daughter.

But instead she withdrew into herself and faded away. Her utterances on the day she died consisted of moaning and coughing; she was restless and fidgety so I chanted over her by the hour, holding her hand, placing my other hand on her heart so she could feel the vibrations of my voice more fully. I told her I loved her, encouraged her to let go. Even with an increase of morphine, her discomfort continued. Only when I chanted did she quiet and relax. I wondered if she was taking in my music after all.

I was relieved when she finally died. I didn't have to try so hard anymore.

Chapter 7
Nathan

"Sometimes," said Pooh, "the smallest things take up the most room in your heart." —A.A.Milne, *Winnie the Pooh*

As I left my counselor's office, I was all into myself, pondering new insights into my life minus my difficult, even mysterious mother. I drove north on Hendersonville Road and turned right into the Atlanta Bread parking lot and parked my car. With my green spiral notebook tucked under my arm, my new red purse dangling off my shoulder, I pulled open the side door to the restaurant hoping my favorite small table in the corner by the window was unoccupied.

Writing here after my weekly counseling sessions, trying to hang on to nuggets of discovery, rearranged truths about my life as I wrestled with my storied past, had become my habit, my respite. Sometimes inspiration led me to compose a first line of a new short story or a poem. Today I was eager to allow anything to flow onto the lined notebook pages. My counselor had given me an assignment to write out ways I took care of myself, a lifelong struggle since I was a giver, a helper and the daughter of a narcissist.

But instead of finding my table empty, I was shaken out of my musings by a pair of dark chocolate eyes staring up at me from my usual space. A shock of shiny dark hair fell down over his forehead to the edge of his eyebrows, more thick hair tickled the tops of his ears. He wore a nondescript orange hoodie, blue jeans, and hightop sneakers, the laces untied and splayed across one of the worn, red and black shoes.

I wondered why he sat there at noon on a school day.

After placing my notebook and purse on another table, next to him, I slipped off my coat and hung it on the back of the only chair, which happened to face him. He lowered his head and began fiddling with a full set of keys spread out on his table like a hand; the percussive clacking of the keys against the table top disturbed the silence of our little corner. A black cell phone and a tall waterlogged Atlanta Bread cup, its clear straw standing straight up from the center of a plastic lid, also sat on the table. I could see the cup was empty.

He raised his eyes. I smiled at him, hooked my purse over my shoulder and walked away to the front of the store to join the line of customers and order my lunch. I could still faintly decipher the rattle of the keys against the Formica table top above the '60s music playing through multiple speakers overhead.

It was my lucky day for soup, butternut squash, a dish I had not bothered to make for myself at home. I rounded out my lunch choice with a salad and a drink. My counselor also was working with me on healthy eating and weight control, other aspects of taking care of myself, and a holdover from my mother's critical eye.

When I returned to my table and sat down, I spoke to the boy. "Is school out today?"

He hesitated, then shook his head "no."

"So you're just absent today then."

He nodded.

"Are you not feeling well?"

He pointed to his shoe, the unlaced one, and said, "I hurt my toe."

I grimaced then said, "I bet I know how you did it." My instincts often led me to such guesses about people's situations. He raised his eyebrows, waited for my assessment. It was October and I recalled my three young brothers limping around with injuries from playing football. "I bet you stubbed it into the ground trying to kick a football."

His eyes opened wide and he shook his head "yes." I felt the space between us narrow.

"That can hurt." He nodded in agreement. "You going to the doctor?"

He spoke softly and explained his mother was taking him to the clinic at 2:30 when she got off from her work—behind the counter there at Atlanta Bread.

"How long have you been here today?" I asked.

"Since 9:30." No wonder he fiddled with the keys and his drinking cup was limp, empty.

"What have you been doing all this time?"

"Playing video games on the phone, but the battery's dead now."

My lunch arrived and I felt silly talking across two tables to him so I asked if it would be okay if I brought my lunch tray over to his table. He nodded yes. I detected a little grin. "First I'll ask your mother if that would be okay."

He shot back with a response. "She won't care. You don't have to ask her."

"Just to make sure I want to ask her. What's her name?" I knew all the employees wore name tags and I could easily locate her.

"Christina."

I found her and asked if she minded if I had lunch with her young son. "No problem," she said and immediately returned to her work taking orders and ringing up sales. She had the same dark hair and eyes as her son.

I walked back to the boy and moved my tray, coat, purse and notebook to his table.

"I'm Robin," I said, reaching across the table to shake his hand.

"I'm Nathan," he answered, still shaking my hand.

When I sat down I asked him what grade he was in.

"Second."

"So, seven or eight, right?"

"Eight." He looked down at the table. "I'm repeating second grade."

"Good plan if you ask me. That way you'll be ready for third-grade work. I have two sons. They were both eight in second grade."

He raised his head, shifted in his chair.

"Do you have a favorite subject?"

"Recess and lunch."

"Of course, all kids like those," I said smiling. "But besides that?"

"Language arts," he said, straightening up. "I want to be a writer."

His comment took me by surprise.

"Isn't that funny. I'm a writer. I'm writing a book. My first."

"What's it about?" he said still sitting tall.

I told him I was writing about my work playing and singing for very ill and dying people. How the music affected them.

"I like music," he said.

"What kind?"

"Hip hop." He reached for his phone. As he pulled it closer I noticed the face was cracked and yellowed, a piece of clear tape held it together. "You want to hear my favorite rapper?"

"Sure."

He concentrated on the phone, tapping and scrolling up and down on the broken screen. Finally he gave up. "Jay-Z's my favorite, but I can't play his music video for you. The batteries are too low."

"I've heard of him. I'll listen to him when I get home," I said. He seemed pleased. I asked him if he had music in school. When he nodded I asked when he could start playing an instrument.

"Fourth grade."

I continued my query and asked him what instrument he would like to play.

"Trumpet," he said proudly, bringing his hand in front of his face, moving his fingers as if he were pressing shiny trumpet valves.

"So what about this wanting to be a writer? Do you write stories in your class?"

His eyes lit up. "My teacher asked me to read my story to the class."

"Excellent. What was it about?"

"Sports." He shifted around in his chair and fussed with the broken phone again.

"I was going to do some writing today," I said as I pointed to my notebook. "Sometimes I just jot ideas down in a list, or I start a story or write a poem if it comes to me. How do you do your writing?"

"I write my story in class and hand it in. And my teacher helps me fix it."

"I was an English teacher and used to do the same with my students." His dark eyes studied me. I wondered what he was thinking. After a spoonful of my soup, I spoke again. "I just thought of something. When I finish my lunch, you want to write a story together?"

The idea shifted his attention; he looked away for only moment and said, "Okay," turning his head back, meeting my eyes and sitting even taller in his chair.

I ate quickly while he fiddled with the keys and tried to get his phone to work. After I cleared my lunch dishes I skooched my chair around next to him, slid my notebook over and handed him a pen so he could write his story. "Do you have a subject in mind?"

"My dad," he said in a hushed voice.

"You can write that up at the top of the page, make it your title."

He resisted, dropped his head. "I'm not a very good printer."

"I can help you." He handed me the pen and I slid the notebook in front of me and printed 'My Dad' on the top line. "How about you write your name yourself. That's called the by-line." He took back the pen when I offered it to him and in bold letters spelled out his name. 'Nathan Lopez' on the second line. Then he said, "I have a middle name too but I don't know how to spell it."

"What is it?"

"José," he said. I took the pen and printed José below his first and last names making an arrow indicating that it belonged between the two.

"How do you want to start the story about your dad?" He took some time to answer this question.

"I'm not supposed to tell you."

"That's a great opening line. Who is saying this?"

"I am."

"So shall we say 'I'm not supposed to tell you,' I said." He nodded and watched as I began writing out that first sentence.

He continued to dictate his story one short line at a time as I printed the words in dialogue style. My heart broke with each ensuing line. I hadn't meant to press him, but he willingly instructed me about what to write. His final line told me he had gone far enough—perhaps farther than he had ever gone with his secret. At that moment I wanted to take him in my arms and hold him, caress his head to my chest, but that would've truly been going too far. Instead, I softly told him that his story was special and that he was very brave to tell it.

"Do you want to talk about this anymore?"

He easily volunteered. "My mom drives us to Texas at Christmas to see him."

"That's a long drive."

"We stay with my aunt so I get to see my cousins, too."

"When will he get to come back home?" Instantly I wished I had not asked this question.

I thought he might cry at this point. "When I'm eighteen," he stammered.

I took my eyes off him and shook my head. "That's a long time."

When I looked back at him, he was sliding the keys next to the phone, their irritating scratching sounds against the plastic tabletop filled our sudden silence. He seemed lost in thought.

I waited, then asked, "Would you like to have a copy of your story? I can't tear your page out of my notebook since it has some other writing I need on the back; but I can make a copy and mail it to you."

"Okay," he said looking up at me briefly, then returning his gaze to the keys.

"I'll need your address."

"We just moved again. My mom knows it."

I looked at my watch. "Your doctor's appointment isn't too long from now. I was thinking of writing a story for you but there isn't time. It's going to be a story about meeting you today. I promise I'll write it and let you read it."

"Me and my brother play football everyday after school. He's seven. His name is Victor and he's in first grade." Why did he tell me this now?

Nathan's mother appeared around the corner pulling her black apron over her head then straightening her hair as she approached our table.

"Nathan, say thank you to the nice woman for keeping you company."

"Thank you," he parroted.

"I'm Robin, by the way, and Nathan is one wonderful son. We enjoyed talking. We actually wrote a story together." She tussled his hair. I showed her the notebook page with his story, concerned that she might be angry at Nathan for telling his secret. "I hope this is all right."

"Oh, yeah. People are going to figure it out anyway."

"He'd like to have a copy of his story. If that's okay with you I'll need your address so I can mail it to him."

"No problem." I turned to a blank page in my notebook, handed her my pen and she wrote down their address in beautiful cursive, laid down the pen and reached for the keys on the table. "Excuse me, but he has an appointment at the doctors'."

"Nathan told me about his toe."

She rolled her eyes then motioned to her son that they needed to get going. He grabbed the phone and stood up, hanging on his mother's arm. He held on tightly as he hobbled toward the door.

"Bye, Nathan. I'll mail you your story like I promised. I also promise to write the story about you. Keep up your writing."

"Bye," he said, glancing back with a subdued smile. His mother opened the door and they walked across the parking lot to a small compact sedan, Nathan's long white shoelaces dragging across the black macadam. I watched him favor his injury as he lowered himself into the passenger seat.

After they left I got up and poured myself a drink refill, collected my notebook, pen, coat and purse and left Atlanta Bread.

As I drove away I thought about how Nathan and his story had taken me totally out of myself. What was the whole story there? Why was Nathan's dad put away?

There was a certain dignity about Nathan's mother. She was upbeat, friendly, well-groomed, appreciative. I was surprised she was so at ease with me, so trusting. Life had to be hard: single parent, sole breadwinner, husband away and who knew what else.

My counseling session, my assignment to write out how I cared for myself, felt like a spoiled-woman's luxury, an indulgence, even an embarrassment in light of this young mother's life, her family, her job. How did she take care of herself?

When I arrived home I hastily hung up my coat and immediately went into my office to copy Nathan's story. Gordon was sitting on the sofa reading but inquired about my day. "Wait'll I tell you." I sat down in my lounge chair with Nathan's story in my hand, told Gordon briefly about my lunch experience, then read him the lines Nathan had dictated to me. Gordon winced when I added the fact that Nathan would not have his father back until he was eighteen years old.

"Hon, I'm going to send this copy to Nathan in a nice writing folder." Already I had more ideas about what I would include in the mailing. Often Gordon thought I went overboard with my enthusiasm so I kept my other ideas to myself and scurried around the house silently collecting items for the package.

I slid the writing folder into a large caramel-colored bubble mailer along with a new spiral notebook like mine, two pens, two pencils, and an autographed solo CD of kids' music I had recently recorded. Then I flipped the envelope over and wrote out his address on the front with a black Sharpie. I stopped myself before I sealed the envelope. Maybe Gordon was right, I was going too far. As I made sense of my efforts, I justified my gifts to Nathan since he had told me of his love for music and writing. I wanted to encourage his interests. As a final act, I added my business card and a hand-written note to him, closed the flap and sealed it with a row of tape for security. I wanted to make good on my promise to write the story of Nathan and our meeting. Life had failed him enough already.

The next week, after counseling, I stopped by Atlanta Bread. Nathan's mother was standing at the same register as the week before. Without putting my things down I took a place in her line to order my lunch. As I approached her she spoke. "Nathan got the package. He won't stop playing your CD. He is so proud of what you gave him. He says to tell you thank you."

I struggled to speak, but I finally told her I was glad he got the package okay. Then I asked her if he ever told her he wanted to be a writer. She cocked her head sideways, then laughed. "No, he only says he wants to be a pro football player."

"Doesn't every boy want to play football and be on TV, rich and famous? How's his toe, by the way?"

"The doctor couldn't do much for a sprained toe but it's a lot better. He and Victor are back out playing football again."

"Maybe you can encourage him to write in that notebook I sent him. Being a good writer is valuable whether you're a football player or not."

"I'll try to get him to write at home."

I paid for my lunch and stepped away from her register straining to see if my favorite table was vacant. No one had taken my spot so I walked over to my place and set down my notebook and purse on the table top. I hung my coat over the back of the chair, sat down and unearthed a pen from the side pocket of my purse. Nathan had been on my mind all week.

There was no doubt about what I would be writing today and how my story would begin. Those gorgeous dark chocolate eyes that captured my attention the week before would look up someday and make a young girl's heart stop. I embarked on my story, scratching away in my counseling notebook on the page opposite Nathan's story from the week before.

Whenever I ate lunch at Atlanta Bread I sought out Nathan's mother to tell her I had not forgotten my promise to complete my story about him. I was relieved by her nonchalance about my slow progress. She certainly had been disappointed by at least one big promise in her life; maybe she didn't expect much from anyone, including me. Making final edits on the book I was writing and having it published and launched, along with navigating some new unexpected health issues, put Nathan's story on hold. I refrained from dumping my excuses on her.

Nearly two years after our eyes first met, I completed Nathan's story. Next on my agenda was to get it to him, to make sure he knew I kept my promise. For a few months I had not seen his mother taking orders behind the register when I ordered my lunch. I must admit that I had not eaten at Atlanta Bread as often, possibly out of an underlying guilt for not having written the promised story sooner, but more than that, a nagging worry that I never would.

Now that the story was finally written, I was eager to talk to Nathan's mother and make sure that using their real names was okay before I finalized the manuscript. She was never there at the restaurant when I was. One day I approached the manager at Atlanta Bread to ask about her; he informed me that she was not working there anymore.

"Do you know where she is? I have something important for her son." He must have heard the desperation in my voice, and readily revealed information about his former employee that he might not have divulged under other circumstances. He told me he thought she worked at a dry cleaners, but didn't know which one. I detected that there was more to his explanation.

"I wish I could help you. She was friends with a woman who still works for us. She's off today, but come back. She works on Thursdays. Maybe she knows." I shook my head that I would.

I made a point of retuning on Thursday full of hope for connecting with Nathan. I wondered if he even remembered me. He was taking up a huge amount of space in my heart; I was eager to make good on my promise. The manager let Christina's friend leave the prep kitchen and come over to me. When I told her about my promise to Nathan and asked her how I could make contact with Christina, she looked away. When she looked back at me her face was drawn, sad. "I can't tell you where she is." Our eyes met. "But Nathan and Victor are with their grandparents and they're okay."

A wave of regret came over me but I took a chance and pressed her for more information. "If you see Nathan will you tell him that Robin has his story written?" She said she would.

Something more nudged me to ask another question. "If I guess where Christina is, will you tell me?" And before she could respond I quietly said, "Jail." Her expression told me I had guessed correctly. Then I said, "Drugs." She hung her head and whispered "Yes."

"How long?"

"Two years. Promise you won't tell," she said. "I could get in trouble here at work."

"You have my promise," I said. "I wish I could send her my love and prayers, but then she would know you told me."

"No, she would be okay with your knowing. I take the boys to see her once every two weeks. She's in West Virginia. I'll let her know."

I thanked her and we spontaneously reached out to hug each other. She must have noticed that I was breathing hard, holding back tears; she herself was stricken, her face gone dark after sharing her friend's sad story. Our embrace felt right.

For those long two years I kept abreast of Christina and the boys with sporadic lunches at Atlanta Bread. Every time I entered the restaurant

I prayed the friend would still be working there. She was my only connection. Nathan's story was burning a hole in my heart now more than ever. I wanted to be an adult who kept her promise since both his parents had disappointed him, abandoned him, shamed him.

I lost track of how many months had passed since Christina was sent to jail. When I stopped by Atlanta Bread for lunch and to check up on things her friend saw me and said, "Look who's over there," pointing to a smiling Christina taking orders behind the counter.

I took my place in the order line and when I reached Christina she threw her head back and thrust her hand over the counter to take mine. "Thank you for your prayers. They meant a lot. Nathan hasn't forgotten you; he's practically worn out the grooves on the CD."

"Seeing you makes my day! You have no idea."

"It is so good to be back."

"I finished Nathan's story and I would love for him and you to read it when you're ready. I'm writing a new book called *Open For Lunch* and I'd like to include it."

In her usual easy-going way, she told me that would be fine. I mentioned that for their privacy I thought their names should be changed in the story. She agreed.

"I would love it if you chose your own names," I said. "Do you think you and the boys might have fun with that?"

"We'll work on it this weekend." Her face glowed. "I'll be here Monday."

After I was seated she came over to my table and we talked about her ordeal. She was forthright about her mistake but full of gratitude for the counseling she experienced while incarcerated. She said she had changed for the better and that her job now was to earn her sons' trust back.

As I left the restaurant, I waved an enthusiastic good-bye to Christina.

I was bursting with joy, hope for this young beautiful family. On Monday I called Christina during a slow time at the restaurant and she eagerly gave me the names she and the boys had chosen for their story.

I re-experienced all of the events of this dramatic tale as I inserted their chosen names in place of their real names. What drew me to this young dark-haired boy? Why did he respond to me?

Maybe the scars of my childhood sensed his young broken heart.

Chapter 8

Darnell's Hat

Our chance meeting began over a hat. His hat. I mistook the company logo on the front of his baseball cap. "So, you're taking a break from eating at your own workplace?" I asked when he turned to see who had stepped in line behind him at Wendy's. He looked confused, pointed to the same emblem on his shirt. Yellow arches with some kind of red writing.

"I work at Auto Bell," he said straightening his stance.

"Oh. Sorry. I mistook the logo for McDonald's," I said, embarrassed by my forward remark, my mistake.

We were near the end of the line so I continued to talk to the young man, trying to exonerate myself and convince him that I didn't mean to insult him.

It wasn't the first time I had overtalked, trying to fill empty space with busy chatter when I'm uncomfortable. As a young bride meeting Gordon's family for the first time, I interpreted long silences at their dinner table as a social faux pas on my part. Surely they didn't approve of me if they didn't enter into conversation. Or, they expected me to fill in the conversational gaps since I was the newcomer. When I look back now I talked too much. They probably thought I ought be quiet, like them.

As a child, silence at my family's table or in our household had meant trouble. My father usually led the conversation, filling my mother in on his day. We kids sat quietly, listened, and ate our meals. When my parents did not converse, the tension became unbearable, the click and scrape of utensils against our plates the only sound. Sometimes one of us, usually my youngest brother, Mark, would tell a joke.

"What's black and white and red all over?"

"That's easy," the next-youngest, Kurt would say, "A newspaper." Nobody laughed, but at least the silence was temporarily broken. We could expect heated words between my parents later on. And possibly a slammed door; and their anger would spill out on us with loud commands, impatience, and a random swat.

Knowing this nervous-talking trait about myself, I stopped my chatter to the young man in the hat. "I'm sorry, I'm talking your ear off," I said expecting to end the interaction right there.

"Yeah. I just started working at Auto Bell."

"Your uniform looks new, crisp. It's nice. Do they supply your work clothing?"

"No, I had to buy it myself. I couldn't pay for the winter jacket so I bought this sweatshirt."

"Did you even have to buy your hat?"

"Yeah, and I had to cut off my dreads to shoulder length. They were down to here," he said pointing to a spot midway down his arm.

"That doesn't seem right to me. If it was a safety issue you could have coiled them up in a ball." He nodded and told me he was trying to make money to support his son, an eighteen-month-old.

"I want his life to be better than mine. His mama and I aren't married and she keeps him, but I try to see him every day." He looked to me for my reaction, then reached inside his shirt pocket and slid out his phone and showed me a photo of a round-faced child with big black eyes and a happy smile.

"He's adorable. At that age I bet he gets into everything. What's his name?"

"Ezekiel Darnell Johnson. His middle name, Darnell; after me. We call him Zeke." Darnell pulled his shoulders back and stood tall.

"Does he talk a lot?"

Darnell smiled. "We read to him and he sometime say the words from the stories. And he call me Dad-dad."

My memory wandered back to my college days when I was a volunteer tutor in a third-grade class at the African American elementary school near The College of William and Mary in Williamsburg, VA, where I was a sophomore. My eyes opened to the ravages of segregation when I toted my guitar and walked through a graffitied tunnel that stank of human waste, across the railroad tracks to the plain brick school with a dirt playground.

One of the first signs of the neglected school was the ragged green, cloth-bound set of readers on the bookshelves in the classroom where I was assigned. I recognized these books as the same ones from which I had learned to read in first grade, more than a dozen years before. Dick, Jane and Sally, white, pink-cheeked, blue-eyed blonds and their dog, Spot, still stood in front of their manicured suburban home. I was sure the only commonality my third-graders in 1965 shared with this reader was the rambunctious Spot.

Darnell had just told me he was reading to Zeke. I hoped the books contained children of color, vocabulary and activities that honored his culture. And that Zeke would be reading sooner, and better, than my third-graders did way back when.

My attention came back to Darnell, in line in front of me. I leaned forward. "Do you want to have lunch together?" I asked on an impulse.

He stepped aside a little, told me he usually ate alone, looked away for a second, then surprised me when he said that would be okay.

Feeling suddenly too forward, I once again filled the awkward space between us with another question. "Do you live nearby?" He explained he lived on the west side of Asheville in his own apartment. Auto Bell was on the north side. "I ride the bus or walk everywhere unless my Baby Mama pick me up so I can babysit early. If you drive along Haywood near Ingles, you might see me walking with Zeke."

Again I had questions, but this time I didn't ask. Having no car made sense if he was saving money; but no car, no driving also carried other implications: DUI, drug conviction, revoked license, criminal record. Darnell hardly fit my profile of a wrongdoer. He was gentle, polite, well spoken. I felt ashamed that my mind had gone to these thoughts. Probably because he was a black male.

"So, why'd you agree to have lunch with me?" I asked after we had been seated and eating our lunches a while.

"Cause you interesting. And I never ate with a white person I didn't know before."

"I'd say you took a big chance for a self-proclaimed loner. I'm glad you did, though, I'm enjoying getting to know you." After a pause I asked him about working at Auto Bell. He explained that the managers rotated the crew around the various jobs and that he disliked the car vacuuming. "I be getting stuck at that job more than the others and I'm no good at it. They ought to put you where you do your best, don't you think?"

"Where's that for you?"

"Wipe down and polishing. I can really make cars shine." His eyes sparkled.

"Next time I come by for 'the works' on my car I hope you're the polish man."

"I do a super special job for you."

I don't know what happened, but I choked up after his remark. I think I had begun to feel motherly, proud, even protective toward Darnell. I wanted to be there for him, encourage, support his resolve to make his child's life better than his own. I hoped to see him with Zeke walking along Haywood together. I wanted him to know I was not a racist.

He had finished his lunch by now and announced he needed to get back to work. "I rather stay here and talk to you but I got a ten-minute walk back to work and I'm on vacuum today."

"I can drive you. I'm going that way," I offered. He thought a minute then said he'd like to walk off his lunch. I suspected he might not want to explain why a mature white woman in a fancy car dropped him off after lunch. I knew that the car drying and polishing crew at Auto Bell worked right in front of the road where I would be depositing Darnell. He couldn't avoid their eyes.

"Then I'll see you at Auto Bell soon," I said. "And I hope you're not stuck with the vacuuming."

He raised his head and pushed his chair away from our table and stood up. Before he took up his tray, he extended his right hand to me. As we shook hands, we both smiled broadly and locked eyes.

"I think Zeke looks like you. And I admire what you're doing for him. Have fun with that little guy."

"I'm trying." And I knew he was. Darnell stepped away from the table, slid his trash into the nearby receptacle and added his tray to the stack already accumulating on top. Then he turned and looked back at me, waved, pushed the door open and walked out.

I stayed seated at the lunch table for a while thinking over what had just transpired. It occurred to me that I never wondered whose eyes might have stared at us as we ate at Wendy's. We were an odd lunch pair, but my attention had focused on Darnell, on our conversation, not on myself. I was grateful to live in a location where unusual pairings were common. Thankfully, some strides had been made since my third-graders, their teacher Miss Jefferson, and I interacted.

As I finished my lunch, more memories of my tutorial experience carried me away. I recalled how my sweet children in that classroom readily sang with me, moved their bodies and clapped in perfect rhythm with the music. And how they clamored to be the ones nearest to me, to touch my skin, feel my long silky brown hair. Miss Jefferson scolded them, shooed them away from me, but I indicated to her that their touchy-feely closeness was fine, even welcomed.

I could still see Miss Jefferson, a classy, expensively dressed young graduate of Hampton Institute, a historically black, elite, private university not many miles from my all-white campus. She told me she had been a debutante. Her father was a physician and they lived in a home on the James River. I knew those waterfront properties were pricey; most of them, ironically, had once been sprawling plantations.

What a contrast to her students, who resided nearby, close to their school in an all-black neighborhood clustered along the railroad tracks. Most of their parents worked menial jobs at William and Mary. Miss Jefferson kept her distance from the kids: she didn't touch them, nor they her. I wondered if I was possibly more like those kids than she was, since I was not from money or high society and was accustomed to interacting with many races and social classes. Growing up outside Philadelphia, all my schools were integrated. I shared my locker, my bus seat, and my books with my black friends, my immigrant friends. We mingled in classes, clubs, orchestra, sang in chorus, played intramural and competitive sports together.

I had worried. Could Miss Jefferson's color, her stature, her education connect with those eager third-graders, inspire them? Did she provide a role model for them? Had I, a white girl? Miss Jefferson, despite her wealth, social standing and education at Hampton Institute, had been trapped by segregation in a school where she didn't fit. I had no such restrictions.

I loved those kids. I recalled an afternoon before packing up my guitar and heading back to campus, when I asked Miss Jefferson if I might use a record player the next week to play "Peter and the Wolf," to introduce the children to classical music via Prokofiev's great musical story. "I'm not sure we have a record player, but I'll check," she said flatly. I still felt how my chest and shoulders sank with her comment, and remembered how difficult it was to hide my sudden expression of disbelief.

The next week I arrived with my LP tucked under my arm. But there was no record player. Miss Jefferson was not at all concerned. I thought her resignation about the scarcity of educational materials, books, record players seemed to match her distance from her students. I was incensed that she was so resigned that this school would be underserved forever; that her students had no real future, no real way to escape their fate, and that she had no obligation to help them. I still felt anger toward her. I had wanted so badly to help those kids.

I looked up from my lunch and wondered why eating with Darnell had aroused these memories, taken me so deeply into my past. I certainly had been a naive teen in an all-white college full of ideas about saving the world. Ever since then I had wondered if my assumptions about Miss Jefferson were valid; I had come to realize my attitude toward her was complicated, wrapped in its own form of prejudice, the very thing I wanted to eliminate from my life, from the world.

The next week, despite my car not being quite dirty enough for "the works" at Auto Bell, I wanted to say "hi" to Darnell and pulled into the car wash line. When I neared the entry, I saw him, rolled down my window and called his name. His puzzled expression gave way to recognition and he came over to my open window.

"How's it going?" I asked.

"Pretty good," he said. "You doing okay?" The front wheels of my car clicked into the moving car wash track and Darnell hustled to grab the large vacuum wand attached to a hose.

"I'm fine," I said, "but I see they've got you on the vacuum." I shook my head. The vacuum began to scream a high-pitched whine. We couldn't converse over the noise, so I rolled up my window and he opened and closed my doors, my trunk, performing his part on the car wash line. I sat there staring ahead watching suds and bristles surround the car ahead of me wondering if the vacuum job more often landed in the hands of black employees.

I returned to Auto Bell nearly every week to see Darnell. More often than not he either had the day off or was assigned to a different shift. After several weeks of his absence I asked one of the kids on the carwash line where he was.

"I never heard of him," the kid said. "I don't think he works here."

"I saw him here a few weeks ago," I answered with an urgent tone of voice.

"Hey, anybody know of a Darnell who works here?" the kid yelled to two other workers.

"Yeah, he's not here anymore," one yelled back.

"Can you ask if he knows where Darnell is?" I called out straining to be heard over the now-howling vacuum, ironically in the hands of a white kid.

The kid obliged my request and shouted my question across the car wash line.

"No," I heard over the roar.

"Thanks," I shouted back over the commotion. I rolled up my window just in time for my car to inch ahead into the sudser. I banged my hands on the steering wheel and shouted, "Shit, shit, shit!"

No one could see or hear me. But I didn't care if they did.

Whenever I drove along Haywood near the Ingles, I nearly wrecked my car craning my neck to see if Darnell and Zeke were anywhere in sight. I never found them. Whenever I took my car to Auto Bell I asked about him.

Two years after Darnell's and my lunch together when I made my usual inquiry, a different manager at the Merrimon Auto Bell said he knew of him.

"Yeah, he's the manager at the car wash on Patton."

That was all I needed.

Chapter 9

"Did you hear what Grampa said?"

My mother called her southern white mother "a nigger" only once. She was slapped firmly across the face and told to never call her mother that word again. Ironically, all my life I heard that same woman, my Grandma Lewis, routinely call black persons "niggers," the lowest of the low in her eyes.

The first time I remember hearing her say it, I was old enough to know it was nasty, degrading. I think I was nine or ten. My family was seated around the dining room table, dad serving food from his usual spot at the head. The "n-word" rolled off her tongue into our midst without emotion, hesitation. My head shot up from my dinner plate and swiveled back and forth between my mother and father, waiting for their reaction. My younger brother and I froze in our seats. But my parents began eating; dinner proceeded as if nothing out of the ordinary had occurred.

From then on, following my parents' model, I accepted my grandmother's verbal designation of blacks as "niggers"; but hearing it still made me cringe. She was not a vengeful person; in fact she was withdrawn, private, quiet. I think she would've taken correction from my father, but not my mother. Even as a child I knew their relationship was strained.

My mother's prejudice was palpable as well, although hers spanned several cultures. Hispanics, Eastern Europeans, Italians, Jews, all were targets of her criticism. Anyone who was Catholic took a hit. And she especially disdained blacks. She had no respect for any of these people. Even famous members of these cultures, accomplished professionals and artists, were assumed to be inferior to whites. For her, eschewing these groups was a mark of good character, education, success.

"Well, there's the old Martin Luther King Memorial," she'd blurt out in a derisive tone every time we passed the tall, gray obelisk commemorating Dr. King near her retirement community in Norfolk. Gordon and I would make brief eye contact, raise our eyebrows, then try not to let out a nervous utterance at yet another prejudicial comment. There was no correcting her. I had tried.

"Mom, there's a new Mexican restaurant in town; I hear it's really good. Want to try it?" I asked.

"No, I don't eat Mexican food. Mexicans are dirty. Food isn't high quality and anyway, it's for poor people," she'd reply.

Growing up near Philadelphia I was surrounded by immigrant and black families whose fathers worked in the nearby factories—GE, Westinghouse, Sunoco, Scott Paper—or on the docks along the Delaware River. She had no room for them, and I was not encouraged to play with their kids, even the ones living across the street from us in cozy middle-class two-story brick houses like ours. We all attended the same schools, except the CATH'-lics, as she called them, who sent their kids to Our Lady of Perpetual Help or Our Lady of Fatima, two versions of Roman Catholicism, themselves at odds with each other.

We were Presbyterians, and my mother was proud of it. She ridiculed First Holy Communions, Friday confession, requirements that females wear hats and veils to enter the church, and the large, loud parties of extended immigrant families gathered for celebrations she had no use for. And she smirked at the fish on Fridays rule, although she was first in line at the A&P to take advantage of the sales on cod, haddock, or flounder. We ate fish every Friday just like the CATH'-lics, but that was different. She was saving money and fish was healthy.

She was hardest on blacks, though. She never had a kind word to say about them unless they expertly waited on her, washed her car, cleaned her house, ironed her clothes, babysat, or pumped her gas. And they better do it right or they'd be called lazy, stupid, and sometimes the "n-word."

My father was reared in a large, affectionate middle-class white family in Niagara Falls, New York, where many immigrant groups resided and worked in the chemical factories along the Niagara River. He attended school with a mix of students, rich and poor, many-colored and many-cultured. His family lived next door to an extended black family, the Browns, who were more like family to him than neighbors. I recall as a grade-schooler that he drove from our home in Pennsylvania to Niagara Falls to attend both Grandma and Grandpa Brown's funerals. Like my mother, he was schooled in the Bible, given music lessons, and received an excellent education at a gifted magnet school.

As a U.S. Marine officer, he worked and went to war alongside multicultural, multiracial servicemen, speaking fondly of them and their interesting ways. I especially remember him talking about his membership in a trio of aviators, the self-styled "Polish air corps": two with long, tongue-twisting Polish names, and Dad, much to his delight, nicknamed Russellski. Their allegiance to each other and the general respect and camaraderie among all Dad's military cohorts crossed all barriers to the extent that they routinely referred to each other with racial slurs: Wop and Dago, Spic, Kyke, Coon, and Polack. The name-calling conferred an odd affection and was accepted without question in these circles. However, these labels found their way into our home and into my vocabulary, since they were used with regularity by both my parents.

The same racial slurs left my mouth as well, but only in the safety of my family and white friends. I was somewhat aware of their inappropriateness, but not fully cognizant of the depth of their meaning until I was a teenager attending school with friends from many of these groups. The tone of my father's voice, his accompanying remarks did not construe hatred or disdain. He did not look down upon persons different from himself. But my mother retained her disgust, her repulsion for them when she spoke; her voice, her mannerisms were clearly rooted in prejudice.

My father continued to tell his racially-tinged jokes despite the ever-growing emphasis on the hurt, disrespect, and shame they inflicted on another human being. As he joked and laughed about these groups, his genuine love for them may have blinded him to the fact that any harm was being done. He retired from the Marines and began working in Washington, DC for the U.S. government. Only then did I hear anger toward his work colleagues, many of whom happened to be black and who he felt did not pull their weight. But those complaints were about job competence, not color.

He was a great story-teller, and it was hard not to laugh with him as I always had when he launched into racial jokes, used his Marine terms for racial groups. With children of my own, his old, but now inappropriate, stories were difficult to endure, but the kids were schooled both at home and school about respecting and accepting others. During his sessions, we glanced back and forth at each other, trying not to laugh. Our reactions together came from a place of embarrassment, nervousness. "Did you hear what Grampa said?" often tumbled out of my children's mouths once we were out of earshot of my father. I used this as an opportunity to remind them that he and my mother were from a different era and that we would not imitate their behavior. That was the best I could do.

The backgrounds of my parents are not unusual for their time, and they beg me to reflect on why I am who I am. But there is one piece of family information that stands out from the rest and about which I remain voraciously curious. My mother revealed to me that her father, Halsey, the product of his privileged upbringing in the Boston area, who married his nurse, my grandmother Helen, fathered my mother, and secretly vanished with his young family to Virginia, took his first job as a professor of math, business, and accounting at Hampton Institute—the HBCU that Miss Jefferson had attended.

What did this mean? Was he truly rebelling against the prejudice of his Boston family? Was that the only job available to him? Had his military stint as an enlisted man in World War II, most likely his first experience outside his social circle, taught him to value persons different from himself?

And how did my prejudiced grandmother Helen accept his work decision? I do know that she and Halsey hired a black woman as their maid and nanny for my mother.

That's where my mother learned the word "nigger." Another curiosity.

Chapter 10

Boundaries

She bolted through the door, fumbled with her car keys and purse and hurried to the counter to order her lunch, her high heels clicking across the beige tile floor. I was already seated and watched her nervously fiddle with her hair. It looked perfect to me—dark, long, straight, shiny, falling just to her shoulders. She concentrated on the menu posted on the wall, glancing up and down between the counter and the menu. I heard the clerk ask her what she wanted.

"Oh, I don't know. I can't decide." Then she paused. "Just give me a veggie sub," she finally said and began digging in her purse. I got up to refill my iced tea as she stepped over next to me to fill her own drink cup. Her sandwich was placed on a tray so I knew she would be dining in the restaurant.

"I'm eating alone in the booth over there," I pointed. "It's kinda crowded. Do you want to join me?"

She looked up, taken aback by my offer.

"You? Sure," she blurted.

"I enjoy having company when I eat. My husband's on a trip to Istanbul, so I'm on my own," I offered.

She flipped her hair back with her hand again. "I'm going to work today; I just came from church. I left my husband there. We drove separate cars and the service wasn't over."

We walked over to the booth and slid in across from each other. When she unwrapped her sub I noticed her hands trembled slightly. She was young. I wondered what might be the cause.

"What's your work?" I said.

"I'm in real estate," she said, proudly naming a renowned brokerage specializing in high-end properties. She straightened her neck and pulled back her shoulders. "I'm showing a house in north Asheville this afternoon."

She was dressed well in a lush green silk blouse under a well-tailored charcoal suit jacket and a matching charcoal pencil skirt. When she fingered her hair again, I spied her emerald earrings dangling from silver strands at just the right length. These were not costume jewelry.

"I live in north Asheville," I told her.

"Where?"

"Up Beaverdam Road about three miles, almost to where it forks."

"I'm not familiar with that area. I just got this job a month ago. My husband was hired by a non-profit and we moved here from Greensboro. We both went to UNCG."

She took small bites of her sandwich, chewed and swallowed rapidly. She fidgeted, like a schoolchild.

"I'm a nervous person," she said. "I've got anxiety."

I looked up from my lunch. "I've struggled with anxiety, too. Panic disorder."

She hesitated, eyed me carefully, then spoke. "Me too. It's awful, isn't it?"

I nodded in agreement and told her I was lucky to have my panic disorder well-controlled with meds and counseling. But I added it had strangled the life out of me years ago.

"I have ADHD and OCD as well," she said softly across the table. Her shoulders slumped. I thought she might cry.

"How are you doing?" I asked gently.

"Pretty good most days, but you know how it can just come out of nowhere."

I took a bite of my sandwich and nodded emphatically.

"My husband's really sweet about it. He's my rock. I'm trying to get pregnant, but no luck. And it's been two years. I wonder if God thinks I am not fit to have a baby. Maybe God thinks I can't handle being a mother."

I felt an uneasiness grab my stomach, my shoulders. I raised my eyebrows, cocked my head.

"Oh, yeah. God decides everything. I pray all the time for God to tell me what to do. My husband and I are really active in our church." She straightened when she told me this. "We work with Crossroads, the ministry helping homeless kids with homework. Mentoring, reading the Bible, bringing kids to Jesus."

I shifted in my seat despite being a Christian myself and firmly believing in helping out in this world.

"I wonder if God is putting me in the role of being a mother to other peoples' children, getting me comfortable with the idea he won't allow me to have children of my own. I try really hard to please God. I'm probably not trying hard enough. It's my fault that I can't get pregnant."

I felt discomfort ripple up my back, my neck as I heard a stern, judgmental, incriminating God creep into her words, a "God will get you if you don't measure up" attitude. Even my face felt flush. I didn't want to hear her words or react by launching into what would become a passionate explanation of my own theological struggles with similar beliefs. I averted my eyes and kept quiet.

My early religious training came in waves of literal, conservative biblical teachings rife with guilt, sin, punishment, self-loathing. I recall sitting at the feet of church missionaries, one of them my own great-aunt, listening to their righteous rantings about saving people, civilizing them (especially natives, in faraway places) by bringing them to Jesus. That was our job as Christians. I totally bought in then. Not now.

And I squirmed recalling how, during prolonged illness in my late thirties and early forties, the neighborhood Bible study women laid hands on me week after week for severe ongoing panic attacks followed by a diagnosis of cancer. And when my ill health, my demon as they called it, was not cast out, I was dismissed and seen as not worthy in God's eyes. That I was not right with God, at fault for being ill. I was abandoned.

Luckily, time was on my side and my dining mate needed to get going to her open house. My stomach churned. I turned the conversation back to our starting point. "I sure hope your anxiety gets under control. And good luck with your new job and today's open house."

She had eaten only half of her sandwich and wrapped up the remainder to take with her. She scratched nervously around in her purse, a soft black Coach bag, until she retrieved her car keys.

"I enjoyed talking to you," she said, easing out of our booth and standing tall. She reached in her purse again and pulled out a small silver case, then slid out a card and handed it to me. "Here's my business card. Let's stay in touch."

"Thanks," I said, peering down at the familiar corporate logo and her elegant color photo next to her contact information.

I could not bring myself to agree to staying in touch. I felt sorry for her, wanted to "save" her, but I had come to realize that was not my job. I guess I could have agreed to continue our relationship by centering it around her illness. Anxiety was no picnic. But her religious beliefs, her emotional illness and her inability to get pregnant were intertwined. I had wrestled enough with illnesses bleeding into rigid religious teachings and their subsequent damage to me. During my darkest days, I felt that God had "gotten" me because I didn't measure up. She was trapped in the same message. I realized that this lunch-mate's story was too raw, too close to mine.

She was the first lunch invitee to whom I had this reaction. It hurt to reject her, but I knew I would not contact her.

Chapter 11

Boundaries II

In junior high school my two best friends, whose families spoke German at home, continued conversing in their own language when we were together. They chatted Deutsch and English back and forth as we walked home from school, or stopped at Shorty's German Deli to buy snacks and speak to him in his native German. They even kept up their German-speaking when we had sleepovers. I began to understand a little German, but mostly I felt left out, rejected. I never told them so.

My most recent rejections have come in envelopes from literary journals and writing contests, but I can get over them easily. As an author and a musician I know I can't please everyone all the time. My mother certainly looked down on my music, my looks, my personality; and some family members don't understand why I write what I do and would prefer I not reveal family stories.

I can't call this next encounter with a lunch mate a rejection, even though we didn't end up eating together. I had gotten my meal and was scoping the dining room for a table where I might set my tray down and enjoy an all-American hamburger, fries, and a Coke. I spied a small table for two occupied by an older woman. She reminded me a lot of my Aunt Helen: petite, proper, erect, with her knees and legs lined up and pinched together; light blue slacks touching the ribs of matching socks that were folded right to the tops of her white Keds. She had a jacket draped around her shoulders. I think it was yellow. She must have just come from the hairdresser, since her hair was tightly curled in ringlets all over her head; I could see pink scalp peeking out between her gray curls. "Beauty parlor fresh," my cousin and I called it when Aunt Helen stepped out of the hair salon every Friday at noon, shampooed, curled, styled, and sprayed.

As I approached the woman I noticed that even her lunch was tiny—a junior-size version of everything on my tray. Her little hands were carefully unwrapping the hamburger.

"Hi, I'm alone eating lunch and it looks like you are too," I said towering over her, trying to make myself smaller by speaking in a quiet voice and not stepping in too close to her. "Would you like to eat lunch together?"

She looked up, expressionless. "Oh, oh. You're so nice to ask," she said in a delicate voice. "But I have to eat quickly and leave in a few minutes for an appointment." She was very apologetic. I wondered if she was so nonplussed by my invitation that she used this excuse to back out of an uncomfortable situation. I hoped I hadn't intimidated her.

"Enjoy your lunch and I hope you get to your appointment on time," I said smiling down on her and then turning to scan the room for an empty table. I didn't feel rejected even though this was the first time my invitation to a stranger did not result in a meal and conversation.

I put my tray on an empty table and sat down, eating alone, devouring my full-size hamburger, staring through the restaurant windows at the unrelenting traffic on Merrimon Avenue, when I felt a light tap on my shoulder. Startled, I looked up and there was my tiny woman standing next to me, even shorter than I imagined. I'm sure she registered my curiosity.

"I hope I didn't bother you but I just wanted to tell you thank you for asking me to eat together. I come here often and I hope I see you again so we can visit another time." Her gray-blue eyes sparkled; I nodded my head to her message, unable to speak with my mouth full of hamburger. I swallowed quickly.

"That would be great. I'll look for you." She left as unobtrusively as she arrived, nearly tiptoeing out the door to her car in her white Keds.

I've since scoured this restaurant looking for her, but I've never seen her again. I can still picture her sitting at the little table where I met her; but what I really remember about my petite diner is her kindness. The tiny woman with the big heart.

When I shared this story with my friend Sandra, she remarked about my never being turned down when I've invited strangers to eat lunch with me. "That's because you're you," she said dancing around, shaking her head back and forth, dismissing the idea that she could ever ask a stranger to dine with her. "You're really sensitive to people plus you're outgoing."

"You're right," I said. "I'm me, but you're you. I ask people to eat with me: what can you do?" I've thought about my comment to her since the idea of reaching out to a stranger, in whatever form it might take, begs for attention in this disconnected, disturbed world. Unlike my usual role of reaching out as a therapeutic musician, a presenter, performer, teacher, I merely become a listening presence over a lunch table. Once my new lunch mate and I sit down, I ask another question. "What brings you here today?" And a lunch story unfolds.

Sitting face to face across a table, eating lunch together, creates a delicate intimacy with no demands, no expectations. Phooey on social media for connecting strangers. The genuine messages between people not only exist in words and pictures, but in gestures, expressions, silences, eyes, movements, available in real time with the person in front of you.

So, if I'm Robin Gaiser asking strangers to eat a meal with me, who are you and how can you reach across the imagined chasm to strangers, to be present for them, to hear their story, to sometimes share yours, to honor the humanity you discover between yourselves? What can you do to erase the idea of "different," "undesirable," "other," "unworthy," from your thinking, and possibly, as a result of your effort, begin to erase it from the world?

Even if I were rejected, scoffed at, laughed at, I would still ask strangers to eat lunch with me. Since my offers have been embraced, I am convinced of the value of taking a chance. When I slow down and notice, I see so many people wearing loneliness, brokenness, sadness, fear, feelings of the human condition, feelings I know well. Perhaps our connection begins there in the scars we carry. When I deliver my invitation I'm saying, "I see you, and I care about you; you matter."

Another story comes to mind when I asked a random person to eat lunch with me and, like my tiny woman, we ended up eating apart.

The Subway was bustling at noon, as usual. I eased my way toward the lunch counter, dodging clumps of dark mud tracked in on the floor on the soles of several workmen's tall orange leather boots. An employee was swinging a wet mop near my feet trying to remove the mess, but he only succeeded in making the floor even more sloppy—and now wet and treacherous as well. The workmen apologized for their mess but then returned to joking and playfully bumping into each other in line.

By the time I reached the young man taking sandwich orders, we recognized each other. I had chatted with him the last time I was in that store and I learned he was working his way through AB-Tech to finish his HVAC certification. "How are classes?" I said. I made it a point to reach out to restaurant workers; they had stories too.

While he made my sub I scanned the dining room looking for an open table or even for a person I knew. Diners had their heads down concentrating on finishing their meals during their allotted lunch time, so it was difficult to see faces. I watched a woman in line ahead of the workmen pay for her lunch then walk to an empty table for two in the corner. She was professionally dressed in a flowered long-sleeve blouse and plain skirt. Her hair was curly and neatly combed. I don't know why I decided to approach her for lunch together, since I tried to ask persons for lunch who appeared to be different from me. I had been a professional, often dressed just like her, in my former life.

With those thoughts, I chuckled to myself. We were different. She was working full-time and I was not; I was wearing gray corduroys, a pink sweater, and sporty sneakers—hardly what I wore to work. Our real difference was our age.

After I received my sub and filled my drink cup, I stepped over to her table and asked my usual question. She raised her head, still chewing a first bite of her sub, and shook her head 'no.' Then she pulled a worn paperback book from her purse.

"My job is so stressful right now, all I want to do is read, take myself away from interaction with anyone."

"I totally get it," I said backing away from the table. "Let me not be the one keeping you away from your escape." I wanted to ask her what she was reading, but knew that would be rude, invasive, and time-consuming.

I remembered my last job as a guidance counselor in a large competitive high school in the Washington suburbs. Crisis after crisis came at me over the phone, through my door, in my email all day long. My stress level ran high. I struggled with anxiety, worry, and carried a lot of the angst home with me.

Lunch for me in the guidance department consisted of a microwaved frozen entrée inhaled in a cramped room set up with a bare, brown rectangular worktable, six discarded wooden desk chairs, a station on a tea cart for making coffee, a groaning overloaded fridge and an old, noisy cast-off microwave. If I was lucky I could eke out a half-hour without being interrupted and join my colleagues in that stuffy room. The noise level was deafening with counselors trying to outdo each other about what had transpired thus far in their day. They accentuated their tales with loud cuss words and wild hand gestures. I added to the fracas as well, thinking this gathering was a healthy outlet for my stress.

Consistently absent was the counselor whose office was next to mine. She closed her door, switched off the lights, and ate her lunch alone in silence. Sometimes I noticed her head was resting gently on her desk, her face turned toward her window. She was talked about by the lunch bunch; criticized for being antisocial, weird, withdrawn. I must admit I joined in that conversation.

Glancing across at the business woman I had just asked for lunch, seeing her read her book, take care of herself, lose herself for an hour, I thought how much better served I would have been had I closed my door and followed my own routine, risked the label of antisocial, weird, withdrawn rather than subject myself to the raucous, noisy lunchroom of my workplace. It never occurred to me.

Many of my reasons are clear now. I had very few coping strategies for managing my work anxiety, which translated to not knowing myself well. And I needed to fit in, be part of the crowd.

How smart that this woman listened to herself, knew what she needed to survive a demanding job. I didn't feel rejected by her response. Instead, I learned something about myself.

Chapter 12

The Eagle's Wings Unfold

Helmer Twoyoungmen was stolen from his home in the deep of night. There was no moon. He was six years old. His mother and father didn't see him again until he was returned to the reservation at sixteen.

"Did they know anything about you?" I asked.

"No," he said.

I sat across the lunch table stunned, my heart dancing irregularly in my chest.

Gordon and I were enjoying a long-awaited trip to the Canadian Rockies which included three September days in Banff, Alberta, a bustling, one-time frontier town now spilling over with tourists, like us, from other countries. Among the optional excursions was a visit to the new First Nations Museum, also named Buffalo Nations Luxton Museum, just outside of town.

Not wanting to miss the museum, we decided to walk and expertly layered ourselves in fleece and hats for the early morning mile-long trek. As we crossed the cement bridge over the gray-tinged Bow River, rippling across smooth multi-colored rocks, the frigid, clean air currents kicked up by the glacial run-off reminded us of brisk winter walks near our own creek in the western North Carolina mountains.

After we crossed the bridge and turned to the right, as instructed, we had difficulty identifying the museum. There was no visible signage. We located a well-kept, octagonal honey-toned log building huddled down next to the river, and walked around looking for an entrance. Finally we saw a single unmarked door perched above stone steps that appeared to be a bit unsteady. Seeing our tour bus parked in the gravel lot assured us we were in the right place. Along with our bus, only a few dusty pick-ups sat in the lot. I slid my hand along the cold metal railing as we walked up the rickety stairs. I felt like we were entering a secret residence, like a tepee, when we pulled the heavy dark door open. Was this on purpose?

Just inside the door the gift shop occupied a typical spot next to which museum goers would both enter and exit. Authentic-looking Native American relics begged me to wander, peruse, and examine price tags. These items were not made in China. These were the real deal and quite expensive, I discovered.

Gordon isn't a shopper and walked ahead of me into the next room while I lingered examining the feathered dream catchers, the wooden dolls dressed in leather and beads, their jet black hair braided and falling down past their shoulders; the silver and turquoise jewelry lying expertly on illumined felt-covered shelves under glass countertops; the trays of arrowheads, fossils; the rugs and shawls, handwoven in geometrics with bright colors reflecting the landscape.

My reverie, a silent, even spiritual, moment among these Native creations, was interrupted by our tour director who bade me and other gift shop browsers, to join our group for a presentation in the room where Gordon had gone. I left the shop and followed her into the room, immediately drawn to a tall beige tepee, log chairs and benches, a mammoth drum, and two men seated in front by a makeshift campfire by an imitation, but realistic, pine tree. I sat with Gordon on a log bench in the front row.

One of the men, the one wearing a brown, wide-brimmed hat decorated with a feather stuck in a silver and red band, his braided gray ponytail falling down the back of his leather vest, began playing a Native American flute. Talking ceased and a true hush settled over the room. I felt my own shoulders fall, my breathing deepen, my mind clear. I knew about this reaction to Native American flute music, had seen it occur with regularity when I played my flute for my patients. This man's playing was smooth, haunting, calming. When he concluded, the other man took the microphone.

"I'm Edgar and this is Helmer. We are Stony Nakota First Nations men. Our reservation where you will be eating lunch is twenty miles from here. Welcome to our museum."

Edgar and Helmer alternated turns at the mic introducing us to their culture. Helmer played the flute again while five young men dressed in jeans, plaid flannel shirts and boots took seats around the large drum and handed each other massive leather-wrapped mallets. The drum was easily the size of a round dinner table. A middle-aged woman a stylish blue floral dress joined them, standing nearer to the microphone. Their rhythmic striking of the stretched skin drumhead thundered through me, amplified by the wooden walls and floor of the room. I glanced down at other attendees' feet to see if they were tapping to the strong beat like I was. They were. I could feel my whole body undulate, rock as the heavy continuous drumming continued.

When the music ended Helmer asked for two willing drummers from the audience. I hadn't noticed there were empty seats. My hand shot up like a third grader who knows the answer to the teacher's question. "Oh, oh, me, me me!" I almost said. He pointed at me and as I eased my way to a seat by the drum, Helmer handed me my own two mallets. Another person from our group also joined the drum circle.

The leader shouted a resounding "Hey!" then set the beat. One, TWO, three, FOUR, over and over; the emphatic bass of the drum beat felt like I was receiving an inner massage. I easily started drumming. The woman began singing vowel sounds, an energetic *Heh!* and *Hah!* created by stretching her mouth wide like an exaggerated smile. Soon all of the drummers were singing the pentatonic notes, the emphasized vowels, as the drums pulsated their heavy rhythm. I added my voice and was so enraptured by the driving music, I did not notice that four women and two young girls in Native dress had entered the room. Their rhythmic movement caught my eye: delicate dancing, their moves measured and fluid with their moccasined feet, their sweeping arms, their shiny charcoal hair swinging with their beaded, leather skirts.

The program closed with a question-and-answer session and a final piece by Helmer on his Native American flute. Our group was ferried to the next room of the museum. But I stayed behind and walked up to the front of the room.

"Hi, Helmer," I said. "That looks like a High Spirits flute."

He looked up and offered me the flute. "Yes," he said.

"I have one similar to it at home. I play it for my patients, especially the ones in pain; and I play out over the Blue Ridge Mountains on the porch of a log cabin near my home in North Carolina."

"You want to play it?" he asked.

"Oh, I don't want to put my mouth on it. I could be germy. We're traveling."

He fished around in his shirt pocket and pulled out a small clear plastic tube, the same kind I used to insert in my flute so someone else can play it without an exchange of saliva. With the tube inserted, I began nervously playing—a Caucasian American playing a Native American man's instrument. Helmer sat very still and when I stopped, he waved me to continue the music. After a second song he stood up.

"Wait. I'll be right back," he said.

Edgar and I chatted while Helmer was gone. He returned to the log bench carrying two wooden flutes.

"I made these," he said trading them for the flute I had been playing. "Go ahead, try them out." I laid one on my lap and raised the other to my lips. I could still smell burnt wood, cedar I guessed, where he had worked to create a wider than usual mouthpiece. I didn't care that there would be no protective plastic tube for this opening. I inhaled, then blew into the flute. Muted, breathy notes rushed from the instrument as my fingers floated from one sound hole to another. I tried the other flute. It required even more breath to play it, but another lovely sound emanated from it. I noticed it was decorated with a nugget of turquoise midway down the front side of the autumn-colored wood of the flute.

"Pick one," Helmer said when I finished playing. Our eyes met. "You are truly a healer," he said. "You have the soul of a First Nations person."

This comment took my breath away. I sat still, looked away, turned back to Helmer and finally spoke. "I can't just take a flute. I want to pay you for it."

"No, I can't sell in the museum."

"Can I give a cash donation in your name?"

"Yes, if you think you need to."

I chose the Native American flute with the turquoise, the breathier sound. Elmer's hand-carved eagle graced the sound hole, just below the mouthpiece.

"The eagle's wings are folded. Its head tilts forward, blessing the notes along the flute. This is the Native way."

"Would you sign it for me?" I said. I think he blushed, but he got up to go find a black magic marker.

"I'll have to write with this," he said returning with a marker. "It's not a permanent marker." He signed his name, Helmer Twoyoungmen, Koskanuba, September 13, 2016. We both blew lightly on the inscription to dry and fix it as much as possible.

"You can get some clear spray when you go back into Banff. There's Home Hardware on Bear Street."

Lost in conversation with Helmer and my new flute, I had not noticed that the same man who had played the drum with me had also stayed behind and was photographing Helmer and me. He came forward to me and said," I'll send you photos when I get home. How about you play that flute some more?"

I obliged, sending the music throughout the museum. People began following the music and a crowd gathered around me and Helmer. He sat quietly, relaxed and smiling as I made music on his beautiful creation.

Our tour guide announced our bus to the Stony Nakota reservation, where we would be having lunch, was departing soon. I stood and shook Helmer's hand expecting this to be good-bye.

"I'm riding the bus, too," he said.

"Will you be eating with us?"

"Sometimes I do."

"Would you join me for lunch?"

"Yes."

En route to the reservation Helmer and Edgar again took turns at the mic, informing us about the reservation. There was a sadness, a sense of resignation in their voices as they spoke of unemployment, alcoholism, drug use and a high suicide rate especially among the young. How there was mistrust of the white man, of government programs attempting to assist Native Americans. I wondered why that was so at this point in history.

They were proud of the new restaurant on the reservation, a source of income for the residents. The building was plain, octagonal like the museum. Was this another suggestion of a tepee? Its facade was covered in sage green steel panels and I don't recall a sign outside announcing the name of the eatery. Inside it was spacious, full of light but still very plain and unadorned.

Helmer and I took two seats at one of the brown wooden tables. We began chatting about the reservation, the current situation among the residents. When Gordon entered the dining hall and saw me sitting with Helmer, he winked and joined another group for lunch. He is like that.

"Why is there still mistrust, suspicion of white men and government programs?" I asked.

Helmer took a deep breath. "Have you heard of residential schools?"

I indicated I had heard of them but didn't know much.

"They came at night and stole me out of my bedroom and loaded me in a horse-drawn wagon along with other children."

He continued with the harrowing tale of the school, run by the Roman Catholic Church, under the auspices of the Canadian government. Education, assimilation into white culture were the stated goals of residential schools, he told us. Most church denominations had such schools.

"But we were malnourished, crammed into dormitories lined with cots. We exchanged every illness that came into the dorm. And we weren't taken to the doctors. A lot of kids disappeared after they were sent to the small clinic. We never saw them again." I wondered if one of the unstated goals of the Canadian government was to eliminate as many Native Americans as they could.

"Did you have any contact with your family?"

"No. It was ten years before I saw them. There were no telephones, there was no mail; no visitors except the bigwigs from the Catholic church. When they showed up we were ordered to smile, sing songs, dance for them. We were all prettied up and a decent meal besides oatmeal, salt pork, and milk was served.

I sat still; made no eye contact. I felt queasy. Finally our soup and sandwiches arrived and I felt better as I began eating. I welcomed a break, kept my eyes down as I ate. Why didn't I know about this abhorrent practice carried out by the Canadian government? I finally looked over at Helmer.

"Was this going on in the United States?"

"Oh, yes. Same thing. In fact, the last residential school closed in 1993. It was in the States."

I shook my head and retreated back to eating lunch. Our empty dishes were cleared by a young female waiter, presumably Stony Nakota, dressed in dark pants and a shirt the same sage green color as the outside of the building. A male waiter appeared and circled our table sliding a plate of chocolate cake in front of each of us.

Helmer poked his fork at his desert, looked over at me and spoke. "And what I've told you isn't the worst." He lowered his eyes, raised them again and spoke softly. "We were abused—physically and sexually. You were beaten raw if you misbehaved." His face tightened.

"The nuns and the priests routinely went down the line of cots in the night in order, from one kid to the next, taking them out of the dorm and back to their private rooms. I knew when it was my turn and usually vomited and cried into my pillow before I was tapped on the head and summoned by my abuser."

I closed my eyes. The queasiness returned. No one ate cake.

"And I'm ashamed to say that when I was returned to my family at sixteen I began drinking heavily; met my wife on the reservation; she was also an alcoholic. We married and had five kids." Helmer allowed a lengthy silence before he spoke again. "I abused all of them."

After his confession, he pushed his cake around some more, then returned to his story. "One winter night in an alcoholic stupor, my wife wandered outside. When we found her, she was frozen to death." He shook his head. "That was the turning point. My kids, who were drinking and drugging, made a pact to clean up their lives. So did I. We accepted the counseling available on the reservation and joined AA. There are a lot of meetings on the reservation. I have since asked my children for forgiveness. We are a tight family now. Clean and sober."

I slowly nodded my head and offered quiet congratulations to Helmer. That was about the best I could do.

"I only wish my wife was still alive to see us all like this, to enjoy the adult kids and the grandchildren." Tears appeared in the corners of his eyes. I reached over and patted his forearm. He took a bite of his untouched cake. We all ate in silence.

When I finished my dessert I spoke. "I'm shocked by your story. Angry about the treatment of you and other First Nations children. I had no idea."

Helmer looked over at me, shook his head, then took another bite of cake.

"Do you tell this story to others?"

He swallowed, and spoke. "Only to people I think can hear it."

"Thank you for trusting me. I need to know this."

I asked Helmer if I could pass his story on to others; and even use his name.

"Yes, it needs to be told."

"You are a brave and generous man," I said.

"I'm lucky. I've remarried and have a 21-year-old daughter in college. She has never gotten into alcohol and drugs." He reached over to his vest pocket and pulled out a cell phone and offered it around the table for us to see his beautiful, blonde, blue-eyed daughter.

"Wow, she's fair," I said.

"Yeah, my wife is German. I met her in Germany where a few of us from the reservation were flown to record a CD of our own music."

I felt my mood lift as good news entered the conversation. A waiter appeared with our lunch bill.

"What do I owe?" Helmer asked reaching around to a back pocket of his jeans.

"Nothing. My treat," I said, placing my hand over the bill.

Instructions from our tour director interrupted our conversation which by now had turned to music and travel and grandkids.

We stood up, sliding our noisy chairs across the stone floor.

"I'm riding back with the bus to get my truck," Helmer said.

As we walked out of the restaurant Helmer leaned over to me. "Hang around when we get to the museum. I want to give you something."

"You've already given me so much," I said.

"This is musician to musician," he said walking on.

Back at the gravel parking lot at the museum, Helmer exited the bus and stepped over to his truck. I waited near the stone steps while he fetched something from his front seat. He walked over to me and handed me his gift.

"Here. This is the CD we made in Germany." As he held it in front of me, I noticed the album was titled *Koskanuba*, the word Helmer had written next to his name on my flute.

"What does Koskanuba mean?"

"My name, Twoyoungmen. Track 11 is called 'Kechew Wetchin.' It means, 'Eagle help me.' I wrote it. It's a prayer song."

He handed me the CD.

I couldn't stop myself from reaching up and hugging Helmer. We embraced tightly. As I pulled away, I bowed to him, placing my hands together in prayer position over the CD. He bowed back.

Nothing more was spoken.

Chapter 13

Sheep's Clothing

Is there a difference between being physically abused by strangers, as Helmer was, or abused by your own family? My childhood ended when my father—pillar of the community, Scout leader, church elder, model employee, outgoing friend to all—beat me. I had been spanked, but this was different.

His massive hand smashed across my face leaving an imprint that swelled, burned, and bruised. It lasted over a week. His blow sent me reeling to the floor in my bedroom where he then kicked me with the side of his foot until I slid part way under my bed. He stormed out of my room, slammed the door; left me screaming, struggling for breath, shaking.

My dad, my buddy, my ally. He knew how to tend me better than my mother. When I could not sleep, his hand smoothed my forehead while he sang to me. He held the seat of my two-wheeler as I learned to ride my first bike. He taught me how to print using his big hand to smother mine and form letters with his engineering pencil. Now I didn't trust him. I resisted his touch, his hugs, dutifully pecked him "good night" on the cheek.

There were two more incidents where he physically abused me, but they paled in light of this first one. The damage was done.

We were a prettied up family. Handsome parents, four bright, well-behaved kids. We smiled at company, socialized easily, performed our roles in our perfect family.

"You're so lucky," other kids would say. My parents told me the same thing. I wanted to be a lucky kid in a perfect family, so I believed them.

That afternoon after the beating, my father came back to my room and ordered me to go downstairs to the kitchen. He sat me on the red vinyl seat of the aluminum step-stool, the one on which my mother tortured me with all-day Tonette home permanents, and handed me a jelly glass of ginger ale, our family's cure for all ills. He never apologized and the event was never spoken about. I recall my mother coming into the kitchen while I drank my sweet elixir. She did not ask about my bruised face, my struggle to breathe. After my father's death, when I asked her if she remembered the incident, she had no recollection of it.

I do recall Mrs. Curry, my gentle, soft spoken Bible school teacher asking me what happened to my face. She may have already observed how much responsibility my parents placed on me, how hard I worked to please them—she knew I had babysat my brothers, one a newborn, the other a kindergartener, during my parents' long Wednesday night choir rehearsals at church. I had been nine years old when they tasked me with that duty; there was no way to contact them. She may have observed how critical and demanding my mother was. I made a point to stop by Mrs. Curry's house for a warm lingering hug and an offer of homemade cookies and milk when I walked to or from church. But when she asked me about my bruised face, I lied to her, told her my brother and I got into a fight. No one had told me to hide the truth. As a preadolescent I had already learned the rules.

Recently, I outed my beating story to one of my brothers.

"That's bullshit," he yelled over the phone.

"Where were you when it happened?" He was silent. "You were a baby. I had a different childhood than you did."

He apologized and changed the subject. I knew he had been knocked around by our father as well. He chose to pack his memories in denial, portray Dad as a great guy, fun to be around. Certainly another way to deal with abuse.

Most of my life I wore a disguise on my face, only allowed my social side to show. But at the time, that was the only side I really knew. Glowing tales of family events, varied accomplishments, my upbeat, outgoing presentation to the outside world hid the truth, the shame, but I didn't know it. Poetry prizes, starring roles in school plays, vocal and instrumental solos, swimming trophies, a Girl Scout sash loaded with badges, perfect attendance in Sunday School, straight A's. The ideal elementary-aged kid.

As a middle and high schooler I ramped up my life with leadership roles in clubs, sports, and was showered with honors and recognition for academics and music. College opened doors to membership as a musician in a four-person folk rock band, acceptance into a national literary society, heavy dating, and weekends of dancing and drinking, the latter a new escape.

Then, as a mother of three children, my energies poured into parenting, being a good wife, running the household, and keeping my sanity with membership in musical groups, garden club, part-time jobs teaching guitar, and school and church volunteering.

This was my form of denial: stay busy and involved enough and the wolf at the door—in my case, shame, exposure, self-betrayal—would keep its distance. At the time, I didn't even know there was a wolf. Mine was dressed in sheep's clothing.

Overcommitment, exhaustion, depression finally blew down my door, let the wolf in, and screamed out loud. But only I heard it. True to form I just tried harder until I collapsed. Perhaps this overdoing explained a history of insomnia, stomach problems, backaches, anxiety. I had been treated for a stomach ulcer when I was twelve.

Confused, agitated, angry, I broke down in front of a friend who was employed as a social worker. As I recall I didn't include details of my past, my upbringing or the bit about my physical abuse; wasn't aware of their long-reaching effects. Instead, I found fault for my unhappiness in front of me, a visible target—my marriage, Gordon. Nothing was right. I berated him unmercifully for not making me feel better. Didn't he get it? My outburst and my symptoms of depression and anxiety were an easy tip-off for my friend to suggest counseling. I went. Gordon and my marriage were not the problems. I felt ashamed.

I'm not unique. My father, the World War II vet, flew sorties as a twenty-year-old over the Philippine Islands. Since he dropped bombs from an open cockpit plane, he witnessed the destruction he caused below, and clearly saw that not all his victims were soldiers. How could he ever reconcile his strong biblical teaching, "Thou shalt not kill," with what he was doing? When the war ended he came home to a hero's welcome for his actions.

He rarely talked about his war experiences except to regale us with antic stories of life on the tropical Marine base in the Philippines: playing volleyball stark naked, trading ration chocolate bars with Filipino women who did his laundry in return; how he had to teach them how to use starch after his first laundered flight suit was so stiff he couldn't shove his arms and legs into it; how a tarantula crawled out of his combat boot one morning. I think he packed his pain up and deflected it by being everyone's greatest guy, a gifted story teller, a friend, Dad and Grampa bursting with the latest jokes, the first one to suggest a trip to the ice cream parlor. But underneath he hurt. His moodiness, his volcanic temper, his verbal abuse of my mother, his other side, exploded at home.

Despite the verbal abuse, my mother protected him from stress, ran the house like a colonel. She did tattle on us kids for behavior she deemed naughty, and we could expect wrath and punishment from both of them, but Dad never wanted to know the details, so often we all suffered for one kid's behavior. My mother herself did not cross him. He medicated with alcohol and overwork.

"You think this was in one of his heavy drinking periods when he abused you?" my counselor asked recently. I had never put the two together, although my lifelong fear of people drinking alcohol seemed to click with her question.

I recall when I was ten or eleven, my mother handed me a sheet of yellow legal paper covered in her scratchy handwriting. "Here, read this and tell me if you think it's okay," she said, then disappeared down the stairs. I sat down on my bed to read.

"Dear Maurie," it began. My father's nickname. I read her careful words about his excessive alcohol use. I had no idea, but my breathing stopped with the news. My father, an alcoholic. My mind raced ahead imagining a blowout fight; my dad leaving and not coming back. Their divorcing. I felt her words grab my stomach, tighten my throat, redden my face. I began to cry. But I pulled myself together before I flew downstairs with the paper flapping in my hand and hastily slapped the poison document on the kitchen table.

"Yeah, I think it's okay," I said and fled out of the house, ran down the hill to the woods and creek, my hiding place. When I sat down on my favorite spot on the bank above the deepest part of the creek, I thought I might vomit. I remained there the rest of the afternoon, randomly tossing handfuls of stones and sticks into the water until I heard my mother call my name.

My legs shook as I obediently rose from my haven by the creek. Surrounded by the creep of dinnertime darkness in the woods, I ambled back to the house, my whole body now trembling with each step. My father would be home.

Dinner proceeded as usual, Dad at the head of the table dishing out our meal portions, talking about his day at the office. I hardly ate, kept my head down, could not look at him. My mother seemed perfectly calm. When would she show him the letter?

I will never know if she shared the letter with my father or if they discussed the issue. Unlikely that she did, since my father raged if he was corrected. The ugly family secret now resided in me; I became hyper-vigilant, watching for signs of my father's drinking, listening for loud arguments between my parents. Ironically, I had learned about alcoholism at our church in youth group.

My mother could swing a mean slap, too. On occasion I could see it coming and avoid being hit. That made her all the madder, especially the time she lurched toward me with a forceful swing and I ducked. Her hand rammed into the kitchen cabinet. For a pianist and choir director, a severely swollen, bruised and painful hand did not suit her well.

"Why did you duck?" she screamed. "Look what you've done to me."

"You were going to hit me," I said as I stepped further way from her. Now I was the guilty one. My mother had a way of turning her transgressions into mine.

I'd like to say that as my mother neared her death, we made amends. But it was not so. She left this world the way she lived in it: secretive, manipulative, competitive, angry. And critical to the end. I performed, danced until I was lame in hopes of hearing her say I was a wonderful daughter, offer up an "I love you," or hug me like Mrs. Curry.

Instead, I just continued to perform for her, up to her last breath.

Hair washing and manicures, music, medical oversight, gifts, flowers, letters and cards, massages, family gatherings to honor her. Surely one of those gestures would pry open her heart. But no.

The loss of her was more a loss of possibility than the loss of a mother. Even now, I find myself reliving our interactions, digging through the past like a beggar for glimpses of love, acceptance, gratitude. If I find a nugget, I make it shine with remembrance of her laugh when I staged my jokes, puns, shocking statements, irreverence. But even then I was trying hard to please her, a performer working my audience of one. "Oh, Robin, you're something!" she'd say with a slight tone of disapproval. "You're just like your father." I was confused about whether that was a compliment or not.

Dad, the joker, the storyteller, the hometown hero, the greatest guy in the world except to his immediate family. He assumed we knew he loved us. I can picture him reading his James Michener books and watching M*A*S*H on TV at the same time, withdrawn into himself after expending energy on friends, community, church, the Masons. Like my mother he also disappeared into himself when he was dying.

More than fifty years after his most brutal attack on me, I finally allowed myself to risk getting close to him. His kidneys, his heart, his vascular system were all failing. He had been patched together with emergency surgeries to the point that Gordon and I kept a garment bag packed with appropriate funeral clothing hanging in our closet in our home in northern Virginia—at the ready every time another desperate call came from my mother in the Adirondacks that another medical crisis had occurred. We'd load the funeral clothing into our car and drive like demons nine hours north. Dad's will to live powered him on until, after seven years of kidney dialysis, and alarming emergencies, his body began saying "no."

I quit my job in the school system in late April to fly to the Adirondacks to care for my father while my mother had surgery for a suspicious nodule in her lung. Gordon and I had already agreed to buy their lake house and take possession in June, but my presence was needed sooner. With mom in the hospital, I assumed the role as Dad's caregiver. One cool, sunny afternoon after his dialysis, I could tell he was miserable. Like me, his neck, shoulders and back carried his stress. "Dad, would you like me to rub your back?"

"Rob, I'd love that."

He sat on the lowered toilet lid in the half bath that I already knew I would redecorate Adirondack style when we moved in. Sun poured through the old wavy glass window as I helped him remove his green plaid cotton shirt. I slathered my hands with lotion; his skin was fragile, paper thin. As my hands began kneading his neck and shoulders I felt his tightness yield to my fingers, which were strong and sensitive from playing multiple stringed instruments. He sighed, exhaled deeply. Then he turned to face me.

"Rob, you'll never know how much I've loved you." Then he turned back around. I can't remember if I spoke, but I closed my eyes and allowed tears to fall on his warm back as I worked into his pain.

I've rehearsed those words, that scene. He was right; I didn't know how much he loved me. Like my mother, he never said so. But that afternoon with my hands ministering to him, I knew I was loved. And I allowed myself to love him back.

On the night of his death, in his favorite knotty pine-paneled room overlooking the pool and lake, in what was now our lake house, our extended family assembled around his bed to say their final words to him. I had engaged Hospice to tend him, to ease him and us into his imminent passing. Each of us took turns shimmying in between his hospital bed and the large picture window beside him. I went first.

He was unable to speak, but lay fully awake and aware of us. I had never seen his dark brown, nearly black eyes so attentive. He stared deeply into me as I spoke. "Dad, you worked hard; you gave us a good life. Thank you and, I love you." I leaned over and kissed him on the forehead. When I stood up his eyes followed me as if he was trying to tell me something. I stared back, and my long-held resentment toward him, vivid memories of his beating me came to mind, startled me into a different presence. Were we experiencing this memory together? I remained fixed and allowed his extended look to ask for my forgiveness. I nodded with acceptance. Then he raised his hand and held my forearm tightly, keeping me by his side. He puckered his lips.

"Oh, you want a smooch, not just a peck on the forehead." I leaned over him again and kissed him square on his lips, caressed his face with one hand. He smiled, his eyes still intent on mine. His hand slipped from my arm as I eased my way out from beside his bed to allow my brother to take my place.

Afterward, I stood at the end of his bed, observing him closely, feeling lost, light-headed. Was it true that he asked me to forgive him? I chose to believe so. I noted that his interactions with other family members did not include touching them, inviting a smooch. I think he did love me.

He died that night after everyone had filed by his bed and said their piece. Expecting him to make it through the night, we had gone to bed, exhausted with his care and the emotions of farewell. In early morning darkness, I heard a tap on Gordon's and my bedroom door. Dad's favorite hospice caregiver announced in a hushed voice that he had just passed away. She was surprised how quickly he let go after she turned him on his side to face the lake. She awakened the rest of the household, and we shuffled to the living room and sat on the sofa in silence, huddled together in our bathrobes and slippers.

I was the only one who walked into the Adirondack room to see my father after he had died. I leaned over him, kissed his lips, ran my hand gently down his face. He was childlike, warm, soft.

"I love you, Dad. Go in peace."

Chapter 14

Facing the Wolves

It's a miracle I still attend church. As a sweet, eager-to-please, sensitive little girl, I absorbed the stiff upper lip of my family's religion. "Be ye perfect, "I can still hear my mother say. And "What would God think of you?" when I misbehaved even a little.

I was scared of God. The whole notion of "God is love" didn't fit, but then the idea that my parents loved me unconditionally didn't ring true either. God the father. Yikes. Later, the chilling idea of God as mother. No way.

In our mainline Presbyterian church in suburban Philadelphia, the pastors who populated the pulpit were strict, Ichabod Crane-looking men in their black suits and ties, their straight, wrinkled necks and beady eyes. They were literal Bible interpreters. Hellfire and damnation spat across the sanctuary.

I sat still and tall as instructed, even when the crinolines under my dress made my legs itch; and often I sat by myself, since both my parents sang in the choir, and my mother was the director of music. Sometimes my younger brother Glenn was plopped next to me, my charge for the long, weary service. From the choir loft, my parents watched our behavior like prison wardens. No one smiled. Each week I tried to skip church by offering to babysit in the nursery where my younger brothers were planted during the service.

When my family moved to the northern Virginia suburbs, they chose another Presbyterian church with similar leanings. I was a teenager by then and could get out of attending the service if I went to Sunday school. My only remembrance is the timid, soft-spoken gentle teacher, a man who wore a gray suit every week, and the couple of smart-aleck boys who tipped way back in their chairs, taunting the solemn man as he tried to teach, and the white overhead fluorescent lights glaring down on all of us, illuminating cinderblock walls painted an unsettling yellow. I felt sorry for the man, even occasionally tried to calm the boys down, but the lessons and his delivery truly were tedious.

In college I dismissed the local Presbyterian church despite letters of invitation and an in-person visit from the young, good-looking youth minister. Instead, I chose the calm, even mystical evensong service at the historic Bruton Parish Church, a pleasant walk down Duke of Gloucester Street from William and Mary. No preaching, no teaching, just music and ritual by candlelight. I expected to be inspired, hushed, find some kind of god in that setting. And I could tell my parents I went to church. I think my mother loved the idea that her daughter attended such a high-class, wealthy Episcopalian church. The soft candles, the music and the silent contemplation kept me returning. Was that God?

I met my first husband, Henry, at church. His family had moved from Alabama to northern Virginia for his father to take a job when I was a senior in high school. Henry, a cute, tall blond athlete was already in college in Tennessee when we were introduced on the front steps of the church during his spring break. We married five years later.

Not even two months after our fancy military wedding, he was killed in Vietnam, a 22-year-old U.S. Marine officer. I still shudder when I relive a scene at my workplace when I learned of his death. I turned around on hearing the conference room door open; a tall young Marine officer stood there solemn-faced in his dress blues holding a yellow telegram. I collapsed before any words were spoken.

Henry's very religious family shocked me by their behavior: they raged against me, demanding insurance money that came to me as his widow, insisted I return wedding presents from them and their extended family, even ordered me to hand over the watch they gave me for graduation. They blamed my Marine officer father for their son's death, a devastating blow to my dad since he had repeatedly begged my beau not to join up. Dad saw the war's long daily casualty lists cross his desk every day at Headquarters Marine Corps. I could not fathom how Henry's family's deep religious convictions could coexist with their hatred, fierce anger, and threats toward me and my father.

The ongoing onslaught of wrath and intimidation from my in-laws drove me, in fear, to hire a lawyer who composed and mailed a Cease and Desist letter to them. I also had the lawyer include a paragraph informing them that I was setting up a college trust fund, contingent upon no further harassment, for their daughter, my late husband's sweet, lost little sister. Henry would have approved. They seemed to back off, but I was left still terrified that they might show up at my door and blow my brains out. Later, I learned that my husband's father had an alcohol problem and kept an arsenal of guns in his basement. After Henry's death, they changed churches. I left church, disgusted, dismayed, disillusioned.

This was the Vietnam era. Even as a distraught widow, I was a target of hatred for the war. I kept my loss and grief to myself, never wore my Gold Star pin in public. My father fell apart over my husband's death; my clueless mother tried to attend to him. I stepped into the role of caring for them both.

"Who took care of you during that time?" a counselor asked years later when I finally collapsed and was driven to seek help.

"No one, I guess. I took care of myself," I said shrugging my shoulders.

That's the way it was. And where was this God of love I tried so hard all my life to please, this being who promised so much abundant life? Bad things weren't supposed to happen to good people. Obviously, I wasn't trying hard enough, praying hard enough. I was a bad person. Hellfire and damnation had come to pass.

I began my first teaching job just five weeks after Henry's funeral: five classes of junior and senior English at the flagship high school in Fairfax County, Virginia. Each class overflowed with at least 35 students; that was 175 papers to grade each time I gave an assignment. I remember the principal allowed me to skip the Marine Corps Band concert at the all-school assembly. I went anyway and stuffed my tears. That's the way Marine families did it.

Keeping my grief at bay became a full-time job. Staying busy every minute was the ticket. I had been raised to accomplish things, stand above the crowd, give rather than receive, another biblical lesson. I did just that: started a Dance Club and a Poetry Club at school, rode the Pep bus to away sports events. Baked dozens of cookies at Christmas and sent them to Henry's unit in Vietnam. Created clever lesson plans to teach Thoreau, Dickinson, transcendentalism, expository writing, to my students; dutifully graded those mounds of student papers, even half-heartedly dated a couple of guys friends set me up with. But at night, by myself, when I couldn't sleep or when nightmares of Henry's brutal death and that vile war awakened me, I was tortured with loneliness and thoughts about ending my life. No one knew.

Where was God, dammit? I was angry, but I tried hard to pray, think good thoughts, forgive my in-laws and the U.S. government. Maybe God would smile on me, rescue me. I was caught in a bind between hating the war and honoring Henry, who had given his life doing what he thought was the right thing. While my friends marched in Washington against the war, I sat home, lost, alone.

I was restless, impulsive. I bought myself a light blue ragtop sports car, filled my closet with great clothes and accessories, ate out often, hung out with girlfriends. I went to Florida over Christmas vacation to visit a college friend and while there made a plan to ceremoniously remove my engagement and wedding rings. One evening, I wandered down to the beach alone, as planned. Staring out to sea, wailing into the sound of the waves, I slid both white gold bands off my finger, kissed them, caressed them in my hand, and put them in my pocket.

With a bare left ring finger I hoped to feel young again, attractive, available, but after the ring removal, I carried heavy guilt. Did that mean I didn't love Henry enough? Wasn't I supposed to wait a year? I had heard that somewhere—maybe in church. What would my former in-laws think of my decision? I still imagined their eyes spying on my every move.

Back at school, after my escape to Florida, I was still a "Mrs." but I wanted to be a "Miss." A very tall, young, blond, blue-eyed bachelor who taught Social Studies routinely held the door into the teachers' lounge for me, often gave up his seat at lunch if I came in after he did. Who was this guy named Gordon? I felt free to flirt with him, but he wouldn't ask me out. I finally made a move and asked him to help chaperone my advanced literature class when I took them to a play in downtown Washington, DC. He agreed. The day of the outing, three inches of snow fell and the event was canceled. He and I got together anyway.

By April I had a diamond ring on my left hand again, and in late May, Gordon and I exchanged wedding rings in a small private service. Running around in my head was fear that my former in-laws would find out, that their attacks on me would begin again.

Gordon held me in his arms as I cried my eyes out during our honeymoon on the anniversary of Henry's death a year before. Later I wondered how many men could do that. Maybe God was looking out for me.

I kept busy with teaching, a new husband, a new house; I joined clubs, we entertained, traveled—but there was no church. As children came along, my level of activity soared keeping up with them and their needs, sandwiching in part-time music jobs to earn extra money, since I was no longer employed as an English teacher. Gordon and I decided being home to raise our children was the more important job, that we would make the financial stretch somehow.

We decided to try out a big Presbyterian church in Fairfax known for its music program. I wanted our kids to be in choir, a place where, as a child, I had found joy, and maybe even God, through the music. The ministers were highly educated and passionate orators, but the sermons often came from the front page of The Washington Post, full of alarming news, spelling out what Christians ought to be doing to make this world a better place. I felt overwhelmed with my life already; now these messages added guilt. I just wasn't measuring up to what God wanted me to do. I wanted to run, but the music program for our children kept me coming back. And I acquiesced to my parents' expectations that we ought to be a church-going family.

Along with the church messages, I felt the stress of Gordon's and my decision for me to stay home and work part-time as well as tend the non-stop demands of house, meals, and kids. Depression in the form of anger and resentment began to seep out of me. Then what I later self-diagnosed as panic attacks took over my life. Agoraphobia nearly strangled me. Hundreds of medical tests were ordered by my doctor before, by chance, I watched a NOVA TV program on the brain in which a woman described my symptoms and her doctor was able to induce a panic attack with drugs.

I, like most people, had never heard of panic disorder and sat there mesmerized. Unlikely circumstances led to this revelation. I was not a regular TV watcher and had just joined my family that night to fold fresh laundry while they watched this program. Once again, I wondered if God arranged these things.

"I think I know what I have," I said to my doctor over the phone the next morning. "Panic disorder." She was as stunned as I was. I had nailed it.

"Well, I'm not the doctor to treat you. You need to see a psychiatrist," she said. I gulped, thanked her, hung up the phone and sat staring out the kitchen window. What would my parents say? Our family did not do "counselors and shrinks," as they called them.

The psychiatrist prescribed a new drug called Xanax. As he wrote out the prescription, he talked about how enthused he was about this newly imported wonder drug that addressed both depression and anxiety. I might have even prayed that it would work as I held the first tiny white pill in my hand before I ingested it with a full glass of water. Even that first pill allowed me to release my anxiety and, finally, relax. Was this how it felt to be normal?

Unfortunately, the Xanax did not keep me in that state for long, so the psychiatrist in creased the dosage with regularity. Over a period of two years I ended up taking massive doses under his watch. Again, rather unexpectedly, I learned it could be addictive—not from the psychiatrist, but from my contextual counselor with whom I worked to undo the phobias which had developed around the severe panic disorder. I avoided locations and circumstances where I had experienced panic attacks: driving, taking a hot shower, performing, going to malls, grocery stores, church, auditoriums. I sweated, cried, fingered icons, recited Bible verses to muster enough courage to drive our son's pre-school carpool three miles away once a week. More than once I had no recollection of driving the kids' carpools when another panic attack took me out of myself. Dissociation, and pure terror.

Gordon was unaware of the disorder's depth and its crippling effect on me. Like a good Marine daughter, I soldiered on. In nine months, without dieting, I lost forty pounds off my already slim body.

"Oh, Robin you look the best you have in years, with all this weight off," chirped my mother. She knew nothing. I enjoyed wearing clothing in the size of my college wardrobe, but I was paying a massive price.

A year into taking increasing amounts of Xanax, following my psychiatrist's orders, I once again self-diagnosed a serious medical problem while watching a TV news program. After Dr. Timothy Johnson, a medical commentator on CBS, spoke of the value of baseline mammograms at age forty (I was still thirty-nine) and breast self-exam for all ages, I examined myself, startled to feel something large and hard in my right breast. That night I asked Gordon to examine me and he too felt the same mass. Tests, exams, and a surgical biopsy indicated I had a fast-growing atypical breast cancer requiring a mastectomy and chemotherapy.

Gordon's mother had just died suddenly of undetected metastasized breast cancer; our diagnoses occurred within a day of each other. We had just been to Iowa to see her and Gordon's ailing father. This death message permeated our household with the fear that I, too, could succumb like that. Shortly after the news, I summoned the kids into our bedroom and we piled into a heap on the king-sized bed for me to break the news. "I have breast cancer," I said, keeping my emotions in check for them. We grabbed each other as I spoke through their sobs. "Dad and I are going to do everything we can to cure this disease and keep our family strong as I go through treatment."

What else do you say to your children, a high school freshman, a middle-schooler and a kindergartner, huddled together with you on your bed, processing this sudden yank out of their innocent lives? Life would not ever be the same for any of us. The sneakiness, the betrayal of a cancer diagnosis, the possibility of another tumor discovery, stay in your psyche forever, whether you're the victim or the family.

Piled on top of the Xanax were anesthesia and pain medications for the mastectomy, plus chemo infusions requiring extra medications for my allergic reactions, my severe nausea and vomiting. Just the sight of the chartreuse infusion bag, one of three drips, could set off the throwing up. I had to ask a nurse to cease wearing the perfume "Beautiful" around me. To this day my stomach flips when I smell it.

Nine months of chemo and I was set free ... except I wasn't. I continued to endure blood tests, X-rays, bone scans, CT scans as the oncologists watched me with eagle eyes for any metastases. With each test my family and I shuddered until the results came back and I was clear again. My body reeked of chemicals. I could smell that metallic odor in my skin, my hair, my urine. I tasted it when I tried to eat. I wanted to cleanse myself from the poisons once the active cancer treatment was over, a way to remove the horror of it all.

I had been on Xanax for two years now, and my panic disorder seemed to be manageable; as part of my cleansing I decided to eliminate it as well, after learning of its potential addictiveness. My contextual counselor had warned me to reduce Xanax slowly since this was not a drug to stop suddenly. I eked away at the massive daily dosage and over a year was down to "just" three pills a day. Then all hell broke loose. Mood swings, crying and anger fits, crazy thinking, sleeplessness, heart palpitations, sweats, jumpy legs and arms, sensations of creepy crawly things on my skin, paranoia. And the return of panic attacks. I wanted to kill myself more than once. Thoughts of Gordon and the kids kept me alive.

Gordon was confused by my behavior, as was I. We had no idea what was happening to me; neither did my psychiatrist. But we just kept plugging away trying to keep a semblance of normalcy in the household as we had during my cancer illness. For the insomnia, the psychiatrist prescribed sleeping pills. Later I learned that Halcyon was in the same drug class as Xanax, and highly addictive.

Recalling my counselor's warning two years earlier that I might want to get off Xanax, I frantically called him. Phone in hand, I collapsed to my knees and recited my symptoms. "You need to call Dr. Glenn Smith at Arlington Hospital. He'll know what to do. He's the only one in the DC area who knows about Xanax problems," he instructed me. I called Dr. Smith, whose nurse offered me an appointment that afternoon. Gordon left work early to drive me.

"You had no business withdrawing from this dangerous drug on your own," said Dr. Smith. "You could have had a heart attack." His manner was not harsh or accusatory, but genuinely caring and straightforward. I was drawn to his British accent.

"You need to be hospitalized right away."

Chapter 15

Face First

On a gray Sunday afternoon, December 4 (I'll never forget), after kissing the kids good-bye, Gordon drove me with my suitcase to Arlington Hospital. I held back tears, trembled as I lowered myself into the car and saw my children lined up in a row at the front door slowly waving to me. I don't remember the drive to Arlington. Gordon parked the car and we followed signs to the admissions desk at the hospital main entrance. I handed over my admission packet to the clerk seated behind a long curved wooden counter decorated with tall thick red poinsettias. I resented the reminder of the holidays. "You need to go to another admissions area," she said pointing down a hallway.

We followed her directions down a cavernous, dark green-tiled hallway, meeting not another soul on the long trek. Our synchronized steps created an eerie echo. We stopped in front of the double doors at the end of the hallway, where a sign above read "Arlington Addiction Treatment Unit." I felt myself sink. "No! This can't be where I'm going." Gordon tried the doors. They were locked. A nurse saw us and opened up, but took my papers before she let us inside.

"I think we're in the wrong place," I blurted.

"No, Dr. Smith's in his office, right over there, waiting for you." I wanted to run out. Oh, God; not this. I stopped my impulse, afraid of being turned loose again; Dr. Smith's warning about the dangers of my withdrawal scared me. I'd only be there for a couple days, I reasoned. We entered his office. After sitting down, I felt some hope that I would finally get relief from the unrelenting grip of withdrawal symptoms from Xanax.

The admission process included relinquishing my "sharps." Orange stickers with my name and hospital ID were plastered on my scissors, my nail clippers, my electric razor. My purse was handed over to Gordon. I couldn't even keep a pen or pencil. I was allowed to stow a $20 bill in an envelope to be kept at the nurses station. What the heck for, I wondered?

I felt like an inmate. What had I done wrong? Was it my fault for taking Xanax so long? I was issued a blue print hospital gown and robe, white socks, floppy slippers, and a tight wrist band. "You'll be here in the unit's ICU your first week," the nurse told me as she led me to my quarters, a single hospital bed in a narrow space with long beige curtains cordoning off my bed from patients on either side. Another curtain could be pulled across the front for a door. I was fixated on her casual words. ICU? First week?

"I'm only going to be here a few days," I said. She nodded without addressing my comment.

"We'll be monitoring your vitals every fifteen minutes at first. If you remain stable, then every hour." She went on to tell me that after the last Xanax was withdrawn I'd be moved to a room with a roommate; and that I'd be given long-acting Valium to override the withdrawal symptoms.

During this time Gordon had been asked to stay with Dr. Smith in his office. After my tour with the nurse, I donned the official ICU attire and was led over to say good-bye to him; he emerged from Dr. Smith's office looking stunned, bewildered. We hugged long and hard. "Good luck," he stammered. I buried my face in his neck so the nurse, standing like a sentry, could not see my tears. I was going to beat this system. I'd be out in a week. Maybe less.

That night the man across from me in the dining area in ICU fell face first into his roast beef, gravy and mashed potatoes. He was disgusting. I knew I was not that far gone. I would surely get out of here sooner than he would.

But as the last Xanax pills were meted out over that long week, I felt worse than ever. I was unfit to care for myself, let alone my young family. Thoughts of going home created sweaty waves of panic.

My kids' short awkward visits were too much. I could not fake being the mother they were used to. They just sat, shoulders slumped, not their usual talkative selves. We had nothing to say to each other. My shame about what I was putting them through sucked the air out of the room. Would I ever be a good mother again? As we kissed half-heartedly and they walked out the door of the unit, I understood why my "sharps" were confiscated. I needed to stay in the hospital.

Later that first week my anger began erupting out of the blue, directed at anyone in my path. I didn't care who caught the outbursts. God was among the recipients. My cravings for carbohydrates drove me to the snack trays where I wolfed down packages of cheese crackers, graham crackers followed by Coca Cola. I remember that the cocaine addict in the unit, a handsome fastidious young black guy, demanded organic foods and bottled water, an ironic twist for a street-drug user, I thought. The alcoholics cleaned up in about four days and were chipper, chatty. In fact, the man who landed in his dinner plate, once he was dry, became my friend and ally. He was a prominent lawyer in Fairfax, Va.

The second week I was moved to a room with a roommate, a young alcoholic furious at her family for the intervention that landed her soppy self in the addiction unit. That week Dr. Smith finally came clean with me, told me I would be staying for the entire 28-day treatment program as an in-patient. "Through Christmas and New Year?" I asked. Then I remembered Jake's birthday in just four days. My throat tugged at my neck.

"Your withdrawal will be the hardest of anyone's. Worse than heroin. And prolonged after you are discharged. Xanax is ten times stronger than Valium. You need to be here." He patted my shoulder for a long time, watching my reaction to his revelations.

"I followed my doctor's instructions. Why didn't he know?" I felt my pulse quicken.

For the first time I heard anger in his voice as he explained that Great Britain had already placed Xanax under lock and key after observing its addictiveness and dangerous withdrawal in patients. He shifted on his feet, then added that the U.S. was allowing it to be prescribed without any guidelines for doctors in the Physicians' Desk Reference, the bible of drug information for healthcare professionals.

Gordon arrived that night to visit without the children. He already knew I would be in the hospital for the duration. My parents had driven down in a hurry from the Adirondacks, early for the holidays once they learned I was hospitalized. Thankfully, they stayed home with the kids. Gordon assured me Jake's birthday party would occur the following Saturday, that he was taking the kids to Chuck E. Cheese's; and that my parents were asking a lot of questions about what was going on and why I had to be in the hospital so long.

"Do you want them to come visit you?" he asked tentatively.

"No. Make up any excuse." A swoon of panic swept over me at the thought of seeing my parents, especially my mother. Multiple questions would be asked, her only way of relating to me when I was in crisis. It was all about her. She would want information, explanations, assurances, so she herself would feel better. "What shall we tell people?" she would ask, her shame for me oozing out of her words like sewage. Or, more likely, she would insinuate that the reason for my hospitalization need not be revealed, but kept in our immediate family, another secret behind bars. In short, she would place me in the role as her caretaker, as she had done all my life, with no regard that I couldn't even take care of myself.

I snickered as a thought crossed my mind: this year she wouldn't have much to brag about me in the annual family Christmas letter. "Robin is spending the holidays in a drug addiction unit," I said out loud to Gordon as we sat in the dim waiting area together. He knew exactly what I meant.

Gordon buffered me and stretched the truth about visiting hours, adding that there was a fifteen-minute time limit with a patient. When my parents did appear, we hugged, my father wept, and when my mother began her inquisition, I was prepared. I shrugged my shoulders as she fired off her questions. After they left I closed myself into my room, pounded my bed, threw pillows at the floor and began to pace, yelling, "I hate you, I hate you." I hadn't ever erupted like this in my life.

A nurse must have heard me and opened my door. There were no locks and anyone could enter without knocking. I wanted to shove her back into the hallway, but she kept her distance, standing silently just partway in my room. "Can I come in?" she asked. I felt cared for all of a sudden. I nodded.

She approached me slowly and asked if I needed a hug.

"Yes," I said in between inhales. She didn't hand me a Kleenex or ask me what I was crying about. Instead, she hugged me tightly and allowed me to access the real source of my tears. It wasn't only anger, but loss, hurt, shame, guilt, fear.

I calmed and we sat down on my bed together. "Do you want to talk?" she asked. I teared up. No one had ever asked me to talk like this. "You've cried enough," or "You have nothing to cry about" were more what I heard, even from myself.

I never felt hurried as she remained by my side, listening to my story. The dinner announcement blared over the intercom. We lingered in the darkness, hugged again, and then stood up together and walked to the dining area, her arm draped around my shoulder. As we parted she said, "You continue to tell your story. That's how you get well," and left me contemplating what I had begun to hear during the required gatherings I attended multiple times a day in the unit. "You're as sick as your secrets," finally made sense.

Besides education about addiction, these meetings, as they were called, followed a predictable format. All patients were required to attend. We sat in a circle with a staff member beginning the session by stating his name, which was the signal for each of us to chime in saying our own name until everyone had participated. We were encouraged to talk about anything on our minds. At first I listened, afraid I would cry or yell, spill my guts to these strangers. But I began to hear my story in other patients' stories, feeling more connected to these random people sitting around this room day after day. So many came from harsh backgrounds—poverty, homelessness, violence, illness, no education. I was moved by their honesty, but more importantly I found similarities in our difficulties with coping in this world. They began to feel like family. I was not alone.

I hit bottom again about three weeks into the program when my rage, my outbursts flew out of me like dragon fire. A nurse within range of one of my rants, waited it out and casually took me aside. "Today's your day," she said, and went on to explain that at this point my brain would be reacting to the absence of Xanax; that the staff would be watching my behavior. Then she added they had the rubber room ready for me, if necessary. I was furious at that remark, but held back another outburst and resolved I would be damned if I succumbed to the disgrace of the rubber room. That day I steeled myself to my emotional turmoil, only attended what meetings were required, and isolated myself in my room telling only my roommate that I was having a rough day. Thankfully, she stayed away.

In addition to the raw emotional reactions, I became dizzy, nauseated, bleary-eyed, sopping wet with sweat, and I barely made it to the john. My heart pounded wildly in my chest, and I craved Xanax, more Valium, to release me into a stupor, relieve the symptoms. Then I wanted to die. Anything to escape this hell. Nurses occasionally poked their heads in my door to check on me. I wanted them to leave me alone.

The only time I felt relief was during the meetings. "I feel like shit today," I shared heatedly. Heads nodded.

"Sorry about your day. I'm not Xanax, but I had my bad days already. It's hell. I'm here for you if you want to talk," I heard echoed around the circle. "The good news is that you'll get better. Just keep coming back," was added. Their offers, their wisdom were not idle talk.

As instructed, I ate lightly, drank water by the gallon, continued to eat carbs, and walked the halls day and night to calm my agitated nervous system. No one avoided me. Instead fellow patients and staff stayed close, comforted me, cared for me. My symptoms eased incrementally.

Christmas was close and I felt well enough to ask the staff for colored paper, scissors, and scotch tape. "What are you planning to do?" asked a nurse's aide. I told her I wanted to decorate the unit's halls for Christmas. She brightened and the supplies were delivered to the meeting room, minus the scissors. I mustered up a group of patients and together we assembled colored paper chains out of the paper strips cut by the aides. After we draped the hallways, even the most dour among us smiled at the cheery edition to our dreary quarters. My depression lifted slightly.

On Christmas Day, Gordon and the kids arrived with two large pizza boxes containing our Christmas dinner. They plunked the two boxes down on the brown industrial tabletop in the meeting room and we ate our dinner on white paper plates with black plastic forks and skimpy brown napkins I pulled from the dining room dispenser. The pizza was already cold from the long drive to the hospital.

Earlier in the day I was escorted by an aide to the hospital gift shop with my unspent $20 bill. I wanted to give my kids each something for Christmas. Annoyed that an aide needed to accompany me in the first place and that she followed me everywhere in the small gift shop, I tossed off sarcastic remarks in her direction, mumbled curse words under my breath. She didn't flinch, which made me even madder. Fuming, I half-heartedly chose gifts for the kids: for Adam, a clear plastic key chain with an "A" on it, for Carrie a cheesy ballet figurine on a silver chain, and for Jake, a tiny bag of M&M's. These choices ate up my money so I couldn't buy Gordon a gift, another source of fury. I wrapped the puny gifts in the *Washington Post* Sunday comics; at least the wrapping paper had some color.

Tension and restrained embarrassment suffocated the room as they opened their gifts. My guilt and shame were screaming, so their near-immediate departure after our measly attempt at celebration, offered relief—mine, and, I imagined, theirs. After a limp hug and kiss, a rushed "Thanks, Mom," off they hurried thinking who knows what about their sorry-assed mother. I couldn't wait to get to the meeting on the unit that afternoon.

After Christmas, certain patients deemed well enough to leave the hospital were piled into a ramshackle white Chevy van. I sat crammed with other patients on the torn, slippery brown bench seat toward the back, wondering what this was all about. The accompanying counselor from the unit explained we were going to an AA meeting. "Oh, no. I'm not going. I'm not an alcoholic," I called out. I was informed that attendance was mandatory, which again aroused my determination to show the staff I was different, that I was being shuffled into the wrong group. Under this resistance was fear, shame of being found out. And of course, what would my mother think—her daughter now attending AA meetings.

The heavy gray air from nonstop cigarette smoking, the smell of strong coffee caused my stomach to flip. The strange assortment of attendees sitting in a large circle talking loudly, intimidated me; I reacted with anger and disgust. I noticed black motorcycle jackets, hard wrinkled faces; tough-skinned women; teenagers in tight jeans and T-shirts with multiple piercings and tattoos, a shocking display for the late 1980s. Some of the folks looked and smelled like they had come in off the street. But everyone was hugged and welcomed to join the circle, including me despite my efforts to hang back. I eased into the circle beside my buddy the lawyer from our unit and hoped I would see that he was as astounded by this bunch as I was. But he seemed perfectly settled. He was an alcoholic.

The meeting began. When I listened to these people tell their stories, their honesty, their vulnerability silenced my judgment. Again I heard my struggles in their words. The Twelve Steps of AA had been talked about in the unit, but during this meeting I started to understand how they might apply to me.

As the last days in rehab ticked by, I became consumed by fear of going home—home to people who depended on me, home where I had to depend on myself. Those awful waves of panic drenched me with sweat. And there was now no Valium to override withdrawal. I learned that the Xanax's effects could be present in my system for possibly two years. So the trembling, the mood swings, and a new symptom, the inability to think clearly and properly sequence information to complete a task, became my new normal. How could I function without help? "God help me," I cried out of habit. But I felt a void.

During the last week in rehab treatment, my panic disorder was finally being addressed by the staff psychiatrist, whom I despised. He was condescending, rude, and even smoked in his office when I met with him, despite my request that he abstain in my presence. My only respite, my safe place, was attending meetings. I still could not introduce myself as an addict or an alcoholic: "Hi, my name is Robin and I'm, I'm … " I finally settled on "I'm a member of this meeting." No one minded.

God was fully absent. Who would call on, pray to, attempt to please, believe in an entity who allowed these horrible circumstances to destroy one of the faithful? God permitted one wave after the other to shove me underwater until I was unable to surface. The AA group kept me from drowning. It became my church. But I cringed when I heard about entrusting my life to a Higher Power, as the Steps instructed. There was no way I was going to turn my life over to anything close to the concept of God.

New Year's Day arrived, the date of my discharge. It was one of those gray-brown winter days when the weather couldn't decide whether to rain or snow, so it alternated between the two, sending dampness and shivers straight through me. A fitting day to be turned out into the world. I was already chilled to the bone with fear.

Gordon arrived alone to fetch me, chatting about how good it would be to have me home, but I easily read the apprehension on his face the minute he entered my room. Dr. Smith had suggested I stay another 28-day cycle to ride out the prolonged withdrawal symptoms I could expect. But my bill was near $15,000 and already our health plan, the big HMO, Kaiser-Permanente, was telling the hospital they did not pay for "drug rehab." Gordon and I couldn't afford even this first staggering expense, since I was unable to work—another source of stress and guilt. Ironic that Kaiser refused to pay when their own psychiatrist had dished out the drug that caused my addiction.

We had no other options. I had to go home. I would attend AA meetings near my house and Aftercare meetings at the hospital, and travel to the hospital psychiatrist for meds. But, how would I get to these meetings, these appointments? Shaky, spaced out and panicky, I knew that driving myself was not an option.

After a teary rehab check out, Gordon transported me to my first meeting that New Years Day even before I stepped into my house. A woman seated next to me, red-haired, full of joy and pep, patted my leg after I choked out my story. "You're going to be okay. Just keep coming back," she said. I hung around a little after the meeting, but knowing Gordon was sitting out in the parking lot waiting for me, I cut my stay short. However, in desperation, I followed instructions from the discharge nurse, and approached the spirited redhead. "Will you be my sponsor?" I felt a small ripple of pride for making this first move outside the womb of rehab. She agreed. Her name was Peggy. She wrote down her phone number and told me to call her every day.

When Gordon drove into the garage of our home, no one greeted me. The older kids were at youth group and Jake was at a friend's house. At first I felt a huge let-down, but then I felt relief. I wondered if Gordon had planned it this way. That night, over a light supper, when we were all together, the sparse conversation sent chills down my arms. What had happened to our lively family?

I clung to life and a pinch of hope via AA meetings and my daily call to Peggy. She offered to drive me to and from meetings after we discovered we lived near each other. She added another assignment to my daily routine, a gratitude list. When she explained I was to write out such a list every day, I gagged at the thought, but she was my lifeline, and I was too scared not to follow her directions. I remembered the nurses at rehab had singled me out a few times and scolded me to follow directions when I selected myself out of the rehab's protocol, or thought I was different or even better than other patients.

No one outside of rehab or AA understood that I was a victim of malpractice, an angry, agitated physical and emotional wreck, not to mention a person floating in deep spiritual malaise. If I took the risk to share my plight with friends and family, they offered advice, blew me off, changed the subject, or found another way to avoid their emotions, their own reactions to such a frightening circumstance. Anyone taking Xanax backed away completely. If this could happen to a pillar of the community, a well-regarded teacher, church-goer, volunteer, then it could happen to anyone.

Meanwhile Arlington Hospital was sending bills, second notices and finally threats about paying the $15,000. After several weeks at home, I began to feel some power and clear-headedness return, so I called Kaiser regularly, confronting the head of psychiatry about their non-payment. He held Kaiser's position and came back at me. "Kaiser does not pay for drug rehab." Finally, I shot back, "Kaiser will be paying in this case. We meet with our lawyer next week to pursue malpractice." The latter was not an empty threat.

Our lawyer, after researching our case for a few weeks, delivered devastating news. Gordon and I both sank into our chairs facing the lawyer, who shook his head in disgust. The Physicians Desk Reference, that holy grail of medication, had no prescribing guidelines for doctors over the period when my Xanax was ordered—just as Dr. Smith had heatedly told me in rehab. Therefore, my psychiatrist and Kaiser were off the hook.

On the way home, Gordon and I cooked up a plan to appease the hospital. I would call the next day and tell them we could try to pay $200 a month. If that was not acceptable, then we were prepared to sell my car. I wasn't ready to drive yet anyway.

When we got home, I placed the rehab bill in my "God drawer," another Peggy idea. She had instructed me to "turn things over" when I couldn't handle a difficult situation. Again, I had gagged at that idea when she introduced it, but I followed her directions and designated my top left desk drawer for this purpose. The drawer was already half-full with little slips of paper on which I had written out my problems over the weeks since I had been home. I found myself praying as I placed the thick bill on top. Then I closed the drawer. Where was this prayer coming from and to whom was it going?

The next morning I called Arlington Hospital business office stating my name and then offering my bill-paying plan. I shook all over as the clerk put me on hold and was gone for a long time. I was sure my little blue Volvo was on the chopping block. She came back on the phone. "You're Robin Gaiser, right? Your balance is zero. You're paid in full." I was silent, now shaking more.

"Who paid the bill?" I finally stammered.

"It's been posted for a week so we have no record of that," she replied in her best ho-hum business voice. I could only croak out a thank you and goodbye before I hung up the phone. My heart nearly escaped my chest.

I phoned Gordon. We shouted over the phone, but then fell silent. "Can we really trust this?" he asked.

"I'll call the lawyer and see what he thinks," I said. Our attorney hooted over the phone with the news. "Just enjoy, have a party," he said. "There's a seven-year look-back period for payments like this, but

I doubt whoever paid the bill will change anything." He and I surmised that Kaiser might have paid the bill without knowing that a malpractice suit was unfeasible. Revealing that they had paid this bill would tacitly acknowledge culpability, and from that a suit could have gone forward.

We laughed that Kaiser just wanted me to go away, which I did gladly, sharing this good fortune only with a trusted few. "Peggy, you won't believe this! Our bill was paid in full!" She chortled, then said in her calm voice, "I told you things would get better." My gratitude list was growing. Maybe, as AA said, there was a Higher Power I could turn things over to.

I mustered up more courage and fired my snotty psychiatrist after I interviewed a new doctor who came recommended from a friend at a meeting. Unlike the smart-aleck shrink, this psychiatrist had successfully medicated other clients with panic disorder. He respected me, listened astutely, withdrew me carefully from the drugs the other psychiatrist had prescribed, and within three months, right near my birthday in July, I was finally starting to think I might be well again. It took a lot longer, over five years, to trust that I could be panic-free—less than it took for me to accept the miracle of the paid rehab bill, even with the seven-year look-back threat.

Gordon all along was attending Al-Anon meetings, as instructed by Dr. Smith, where a similar format allowed him to tell his story and receive the same honest caring that could bring him healing. We heard in our meetings that addiction was a family disease. Now tentatively driving, I was faithfully showing up, often to two of my own meetings a day, and going out for coffee or lunch with new AA friends, the meeting after the meeting, as we called it. Life was coming back, dinner table conversation with the family had become lively again. A calm, level-headed mother who actively worked the processes of the Twelve Steps was emerging, actually getting well. Gordon was also applying the Steps to his life so the children were beneficiaries of our combined recovery.

Many amends were made. I found family counseling excruciating as I heard the kids pour out their truths, their experiences with a mother whacked out on Xanax: their embarrassment, their anger, their shame over my addiction and rehab. But in order for healing to occur, I knew we all had to share our secrets. During follow-up rehab sessions at Aftercare, in private, my counselor gently helped me untangle the masses of pent-up emotions finally coming to the surface in our family.

I decided to try out church with the family again, allowing myself to "take what I needed and leave the rest," another piece of AA wisdom. The kids were still singing in choirs, and I hated to miss the church music, still a source of spiritual connection for me. Since the words to the church music and liturgies often contained theology that hurt, I concentrated on singing the melodies and ignored most of the lyrics, recited the liturgies by rote when I felt like it. There was a measure of comfort in the familiar, but so many messages in church just did not apply to me anymore. My kids lovingly called me the Christian Buddhist, following my own "right path."

I had come to believe finally that God did not deliver hellfire and damnation; illness, death, tragedy, disaster were natural outcomes of living in a flawed world, a flawed body. I was not a bad person.

I was erasing the notion that miracles, good things happened because I pleased God. Instead, a more expansive, inclusive sense of God entered my theology. Life was not a favor/reward system, a black and white if/then logic. I actually started to believe that a Higher Power did exist and that it could love me, faults and all. Gordon had certainly demonstrated that to me.

One day, while sitting at my desk, I was drawn to my God drawer. When I eased the drawer out, all the little scraps of paper where I continued to write out my troubles and turn them over to God, puffed up out of the drawer and nearly overflowed. I scooped up a pile and dumped it on my lap. As I read the scribbled concerns, my untenable worries, I realized that each one had been resolved in its own mysterious way. But most often not in the way I had expected.

How? By whom?

A mystery. A holy mystery. God as Holy Mystery. Not miracles, but mysteries. I could live with that. I sat looking out the window to the woods behind our house, the pile of answered prayers falling one by one off my lap to the floor.

Over the years, despite my life taking a big turn toward wellness, despite loving myself, despite forgiving myself and others, old habits still surface, linger, hold me down. I want an easy fix, a tsunami, a mountain-top experience to change me. If I work harder on myself, read all the newest self-help books, pray more, follow directions of counselors, healers, I could make this happen. But when I think and act this way, something familiar creeps over me.

I hear Peggy's voice. "Take it easy, let go and let God," she often said. "Overworking, overachieving, over-analysis, impatience, and expecting outcomes have gotten you into trouble in the past."

I am reminded regularly to back down, breathe, and allow the slow, holy mysteries of healing, loving, forgiving, to unfold over time, in their own time.

Lots of time.

Chapter 16

Perfect Harmony

"Everything can be taken from a man, but one thing; the last of human freedoms—to choose one's attitude in any given set of circumstances, to choose one's own way." —Viktor Frankl, *Man's Search for Meaning*

Luella's Barbecue, a funky reimagined restaurant on Merrimon Avenue in Asheville, grabbed my hunger attention with the scent of smoked meat sneaking in my partly-opened sunroof. The former drive-in eatery now housed a popular dining spot for locals and tourists. As I drove into the parking lot, my Sirius station rocked out music from channel 32, The Bridge, where James Taylor happened to be playing. I sang along. *In my mind I'm goin' to Carolina*. Perhaps the sunroof let out a little of James's exuberance. I was starving and I was by myself.

The ordering line was long, but efficient. I was second in line in no time. A young guy stood in front of me at the counter and gave his order to a young blonde, dreadlocked, multi-pierced woman sporting a black Luella's tee shirt and large black-framed glasses. Before he stepped away from the counter, the notion hit me, as it so often does, so I spoke to him. "Hi, I'm alone for lunch, would you like to eat together?" He turned to face me, then backed away, wrinkled his brow, gave me the once-over.

"Oh, no. Not that," I said. "I'm only asking for lunch. I'm married, a mother, a grandmother, a church-goer." He stood still, studying me up and down, then looked into my eyes. I smiled. He finally agreed to my offer. I spotted an empty table and pointed my finger that way. "That one okay?" I asked.

"Sure."

It was then that I noticed his cane, leaning against the tall stocky bar where we stood to order. Military: Iraq, Afghanistan; a young victim of these horrible wars. But his cane was not a four-footed aluminum device, the type issued by physical therapists, hospitals, like the ones I saw in my patients' rooms. This cane was beautiful: wooden, elaborately carved, likely handmade. He slid his hand down and caressed the cane's curved handle, steadied himself and moved sideways away from the counter. I watched him squeeze his way through the crowd to our chosen table, a tall blue plastic drink cup and order number rocking back and forth with his gait.

"Can I take your order, please?" The blonde startled me back to the order counter. I chose my usual pulled barbecue chicken sandwich with a side of vinegar slaw, drained. The vinegar dressing made me choke and cough if I swallowed too much of it. I guess I was still only a Carolina girl "in my mind" if I couldn't handle a southern staple food, although I had come to love collards and hush puppies. With my order number in my hand, plus my drink cup, I sidled through the crowded tables over to where my lunch mate now sat. His drink cup sat next to his order number. It was empty.

"I need to fill my own cup. Can I get your drink for you?"

"Oh, okay. Just water," he said.

Pandering to a young disabled stranger might have met resistance. Especially a young guy. And a very handsome one at that. Strong jaw, large brown-black eyes, and a thick shock of dark hair combed to the side, like some movie star I couldn't put a name to. He wore stylish, angular charcoal-colored glasses. He had removed a suede leather jacket and draped it over the back of his chair. A neatly-pressed, well-fitting dress shirt and khakis completed his look.

I left the table to fill our drinking glasses at the nearby dispenser, then returned to our table and set them down next to our order numbers.

"Thanks," he said. "I'm Kevin Kross," and reached across the table to shake hands. I shared my name and my hand and sat down, removing my red down vest and hooking it on the corner of my chair. I scraped the chair legs across the floor as I pulled in closer to the table. The continuous squeal of aluminum chairs against the cement floor was an ongoing intrusion into conversation at Luella's.

"What brings you here today?" I asked.

"I work nearby and I like to eat here once a week. I'm careful about my diet. Maybe you noticed I'm limping today."

I had to tell the truth. I had noticed, even though not mentioning it was what I often assumed someone might prefer. It was awkward to pretend, however.

"I have MS," Kevin said. "I was diagnosed at twenty-one." He was no pretender. He told me he was twenty-three, an accountant at Nantahala. He was well-spoken. And engaged to be married in three months. "I've given Jenny every out for this marriage. But she won't leave me. She insists. We want a house, a family, to be as normal as possible."

I looked into his eyes as he shared this striking detail. He was steady, serious. What would I do? A debilitating illness. Progressive. Incurable. And they were young, so Multiple Sclerosis would dictate their lifestyle for as long as Kevin lived. And how long would that be?

"I've been doing really well but I've had a setback. Stress will do that to me, make my weakness and trembling worse. Please excuse me if I make a mess eating my lunch. My hands are so unsteady today."

He lowered his head, looked at his full plate of chicken, collards and slaw. "My grandparents died a day apart five days ago. Grandpa and Grandma sat next to each other in the living room for as long as I can remember. We lived next door. Did you see my cane? My Grandpa made it for me." He looked up at me. "I can't go to their house and see the empty chairs." He stammered with these last words.

"That's a lot, all at once. I'm sorry."

He fumbled with his fork and finally stabbed a piece of chicken; his hand shook as he put it in his mouth. When he had chewed and swallowed his food, he changed the subject. "What brought you here today?"

"I just played and sang for an elderly friend at the Baptist Home. She's in pain and the music helps her relax, even lose the pain. She's ninety-nine."

"Is that a job or do you go as a friend?"

"A little of both. I'm a Certified Music Practitioner and sometimes I'm hired, but since we moved to Asheville I'm mostly volunteering. I prefer the freedom."

He asked about the CMP designation, what I did, what kind of education it took to do this kind of work, then we both let conversation lapse to eat our lunches. I tried not to notice as his fork jittered when he attempted to bring a piece of chicken to his mouth. Often his food fell back down to his plate, the table or his lap. He hardly got much of it eaten.

Despite noticing his dilemma, I did not offer to assist him with his lunch. I could have cut his meat into smaller pieces so he could scoop it up with a spoon. His determination to push through his life circumstances, marry, have a family, go to work, own a home, was powerful, so I kept still until he volunteered to talk. "I'll take most of my lunch home for later," he said as if to justify his inability to get food to his mouth. I wondered if he ate with his hands when he was not out in public. He continued his effort at eating, chewing each bite slowly—a good thing. He knew MS came with choking hazards.

He looked up again, and stopped eating. "I went to Panama for stem-cell therapy. I couldn't even walk when I went. Using a cane is unusual for me now. But I'll get stronger. I'm not worried. The treatments were $25,000. A friend convinced me to write up my story on GO FUND ME and the money just rolled in."

"You have an amazing story," I said. "Have you considered writing it?" After that comment I felt stupid. If he could hardly eat, how could he write? I wrote in long hand before I entered my work into a computer. Then I remembered, he was an accountant, and that work required more than paper and pencil these days. He would have to be computer-literate. How easy it was to make assumptions.

"Wait till you hear the rest," he said, straightening up in his chair, pulling back and squaring his shoulders. "When I went to pay my bill at the clinic, someone had already paid the whole $25,000. I don't know who it was, but I have an idea."

Now I sat up straight, pulling my shoulders back. "That sounds like a miracle. Wow. There's a great story there."

"Yep. And so I still have money enough for another treatment in Panama. That is, if I need one."

Kevin's enthusiasm, hope, and determination infused me with joy and affection for my newly-found lunch mate. My love for him, my desire to help in any way prompted me to ask him a question.

"Do you like music?"

"Oh, yeah. All kinds. Right now, no heavy metal. Too crazy. I need to be as calm as possible." I resonated with that comment, realizing how much I also craved peace and quiet to maintain my own calmness.

"Do you play an instrument or sing?"

"I like to sing to the radio, but no instruments. I wanted to, but I never tried it. Guitar, you know, be a rock star."

"Every teenager who walked through my music studio door with a guitar in hand had that same dream." Our eyes met and we smiled.

"How's the strength in your left hand? Can you push and hold with one finger?" He held his left hand up and pointed a straight index finger in the air almost asking me to make an evaluation of his ability. I nodded.

"Can you hold a thick medium-sized thick pick with your right hand?" This time he raised his right hand and simulated pinching a pick between his thumb and forefinger. He cocked his head, his eyes searching me for where I was going with this quiz.

"I think you can play the autoharp."

He looked up and beyond me. Maybe he was trying to imagine himself making music, or how this instrument might sound. Then he surprised me.

"I'm not sure what an autoharp is."

I had mistakenly assumed everyone experienced an elementary music teacher pushing the white chord buttons on the autoharp, and strumming across the strings with a thick gray felt pick, accompanying small voices singing "Oh, Susanna" or "My Country, 'Tis of Thee."

I described the instrument to Kevin, emphasizing that it would be ideal since it could be played lying flat on a table. "The music of this instrument is calming, soothing. Straight to the heart. It might lessen your stress."

"I don't know how to read music," he said, nearly apologizing.

"There's the other beauty. You don't have to."

He took a deep breath and grinned. "I think I'd like to give it a try. Where can I get an autoharp?"

"Funny, but I was just given a second autoharp by a friend. You can borrow it."

He gazed up and over me again, then looked down at his unfinished lunch. "Oh, gosh, I need a box for my food and I need to get back to work." He hailed a waiter as I reached for my purse and rustled around inside it to find my business cards. I slid one across the table to him.

"If you still want to try this we need to get together, I think, so I can hand you the autoharp and give you some tips on playing. My card has my email and phone." He took up my card in his hand and began reading it.

"You didn't tell me you were also a writer. No wonder you suggested I write my story."

"We can talk about that another time since you need to get going."

"That sounds good. I'll email you," he said.

The waiter arrived at our table and slid Kevin's lunch from his plate into a carry-out box. I was thankful this task was done for him even though I would've taken the liberty to help out with this chore.

Kevin was shaky when he stood up. He slipped my card into his shirt pocket, reached around for his jacket, and methodically slid one arm then the other down the satin-lined arms of each supple sleeve. He didn't zip his jacket, even though early spring still held daytime temperatures in the 40s. I did not offer to do this for him. That would have been too personal, too motherly.

"I'll be in touch," he said lifting his box of leftovers from the table with both hands, then shifting it to one hand and grasping his cane with the other. He shimmied between tables and then turned his back to me, steadying himself and working his way toward the front door. I was ready to jump up and hold the door for him but a kind soul entering Luella's kept the door wide open as he stepped out.

I twisted my body so I could see him through Luella's front window. I was still in caretaker mode. He surprised me again when he approached a low-slung, snazzy metallic blue coupe parked in a handicap space outside the front door. He placed his food box on the hood, opened the driver's door and lowered himself into the seat. I had to smile. Why was I surprised that Kevin drove a sports car?

I collected my purse and vest and left the restaurant to drive home. When I pushed my garage door opener I wondered how I had gotten from the restaurant to my home so quickly. Lost in Kevin's story, I didn't recall any of the six-mile drive.

Gordon was absorbed in his computer when I greeted him. Despite the urge to interrupt him with my latest lunch encounter, I decided to wait until he was fully present for the story. And anyway, I wanted time to sit with the experience. First, I checked my emails. There was already a message from Kevin.

"I enjoyed meeting you. When can we get together?"

He certainly didn't waste any time. Under other circumstances I might have been the person sizing him up, evaluating this rapid response. But Kevin had no time to waste.

I conjured up a plan to invite Kevin and Jenny over for dessert some evening. Just who was this extraordinary young woman who was pledging her love and loyalty to Kevin under the most dire of circumstances? I wanted to meet her, even size her up. I felt a certain protectiveness toward Kevin. He was a dichotomy of toughness and fragility. Over dinner I told Gordon the Kevin story and suggested the dessert plan. He welcomed the idea, expressing the same combination of admiration and curiosity about this young couple

Kevin responded to my email invitation and we decided to meet the next Friday evening. Meanwhile, I tuned the autoharp to ensure the most pleasing sounds would envelop Kevin when he pulled the new gray felt pick I purchased for him across the strings for the first time. Hopefully, he would not only hear the perfect harmony, but feel the vibration all over and through his ailing body, into his grief over his grandparents' deaths.

Kevin and Jenny arrived on time, comfortably introducing themselves and removing coats. Jenny automatically took Kevin's jacket and handed both hers and his to Gordon when he offered to hang them in our coat closet. She looked like I expected her to look. Medium build, a little shorter than Kevin, neatly dressed in jeans and a yellow sweater. Her hair was somewhat long but nicely styled, wavy brown. Her eyes, a bright blue, really spoke to me—serious, straightforward, observant. I led them to our great room to sit in a cozy corner of sofas and lounge chairs near the fire Gordon had stoked in the stone fireplace.

I spoke first after we all found our seats. Jenny and Kevin sat close together on the soft green sofa facing the fire. "Jenny, what's your line of work?" Her face brightened when she told me about her work as an occupational therapy assistant, how it helped her care for Kevin. "But," she added, "we're saving money for me to get my Masters in OT at Western Carolina University. I've already applied for next fall." Kevin put his arm around her and vehemently nodded.

"Occupational Therapy is an ambitious career these days. Lots more requirements than when I was looking at it forty years ago. Back in the day all you had to have was a BS for OT or PT. Now PT requires a doctorate. Do you think OT will follow suit?" Jenny looked surprised that I knew this.

"I want to get in the door before the requirements change. Working in the field as an assistant I hope will help me get in. And with some scholarship money. My supervisors have agreed to write my letters of recommendation."

"She didn't tell you she had a 4.0 as an undergrad and got really good GRE scores." Then he added, "And we're saving for a house, too. We know what we want—a one-story rancher out near my family in Candler. At least three bedrooms. We want to have children." He beamed as he spoke.

I sat there stunned by the mature planning, the hard work, the ambitions these two shared. How many young twenty-somethings without Kevin and Jenny's obstacles behaved this way? But then, I thought how my own obstacles throughout my life had resulted in an accelerated determination to get on with living, make my dreams happen.

The loving exchanges between Kevin and Jenny confirmed my belief that the world was full of truly good people. They were not pretenders.

"So, a wedding in May?" asked Gordon. A ripple of excitement made them both squirm.

"Yep, May 3," Kevin chirped. "Oh, gosh, I need to be fitted for my tux by the end of this month," he said looking over to Jenny. She acknowledged his comment with a small nod of her head, but offered no advice or assistance. I imagine she knew the fine line between enabling Kevin and supporting him.

"We're having the wedding outside. We hope," Kevin said wide-eyed. "We rented a tent just in case, but we want to have room to dance. We've hired a great DJ and have arranged for a food truck come to do the catering."

Jenny chimed in, "That way each person can order what they want and everything will be fresh and healthy. We watch what we eat."

Gordon and I turned to each other shaking our heads. "Here's to the best day ever," Gordon said raising both his hands, palms up. Jenny continued explaining that they sent out one hundred invitations, the maximum number of guests they could afford, and so far everyone was coming. Secretly I wanted to attend.

I suggested we have some dessert. Kevin and I had agreed on what I would serve to honor their habit of eating well. As I disappeared into the kitchen I felt a sense of sadness interfere with my joy about this couple. They were so pragmatic. I wanted them to be more free, more like young lovers; even foolish and giddy.

From a distance I could hear Gordon talking to our guests, but I was unable to decipher just what he said. He tended to hold back from conversation when I was present, let me be the social one. Talking to strangers is not his forte.

He joined me in the kitchen to prepare mugs of coffee for all of us. I left him there and entered the great room with a tray bearing four plates, each laden with a warm brownie, a small scoop of vanilla ice cream and a drizzle of Hershey's syrup. I had included spoons for the food in hopes Kevin would be more comfortable eating. Gordon followed me with the coffee.

The fire continued to roar as our comfortable foursome lapped up our desserts in silence except for the scraping of spoons across the plates to capture every drop of chocolate syrup. Kevin was able to feed himself the dessert without making a mess.

"While we enjoy coffee, let's get to this autoharp adventure," I said, rising to walk to the dining room table where the instrument lay flat, still in its case. An assortment of music books from my collection, each one with a different approach to playing autoharp without needing to read music, was piled near the autoharp.

"I noticed that black case and some music over there. Is that for me?" Kevin said as he got up and followed me to the dining room using only the furniture to steady himself. Jenny brought his cane along and carried his coffee mug, then stood nearby as he pulled out a chair to seat himself at the table. Once he was seated, she stood behind him. I sat next to Kevin and Gordon stood to my side. I dramatized the moment by stalling a few seconds before I clicked open the three clasps on the case, slowly raised the lid and unveiled the autoharp. It gleamed—freshly dusted, shiny, and finely tuned.

"So, that's an autoharp," Kevin said. I removed it from its case and laid it on the table in front of him. He studied it, but didn't touch it.

"This thing can be heavy, that's the only drawback, so leaving it on the table to play would be best. But, here, press this button marked 'C' with your left index finger." He tentatively pushed down on the chord button. Next, I handed him a thick gray felt pick. "Now hold the pick between your thumb and index finger on your right hand and strum all the way across the strings." Kevin looked back at Jenny, then over at me before he followed my instructions. When he dragged the large plectrum across the full length of the autoharp strings and created a beautiful chord right away, he shivered, grinned broadly. As he continued to strum the C chord, Jenny gently squeezed his shoulders, smiling down at her fiancé's accomplishment.

I kept silent and let him produce glorious, heavenly music on the instrument, strum after strum. "You can push down any button you want. The trick is to just firmly hold down because the button is actually holding the whole chord bar across the strings." I pointed to the side of a visible chord bar. Kevin and Jenny tilted their heads to examine the mechanism.

"I'm learning some things too," Gordon said as he bent down to see how things worked. Kevin pushed more buttons and strummed random cords one after the other, making his own music. No rules. Total improvisation. And beautiful.

As he played, I recalled how my mother nearly ruined my musical spark for improvisation and playing by ear. For her, reading music, recreating the printed score, was the only real way to make music. And, to her, classical music was the highest order of musical genre. How would my mother have reacted to Kevin's music? My instruction?

With unsettling memories of her rigid, angry pronouncements about my music-making, I vowed to never inflict that on anyone. When my own children showed interest in music lessons, I carefully chose their teachers, and allowed them to discover the joy in their own playing. During their childhood, I gave lessons in our special in-home, sound-proof studio, a place where they could also practice on their own, make their own music. A place I had wished for as a kid.

As Kevin sat beside me, playing his own music, his jaw, his arms, his shoulders relaxed. I imagined the stress melting away from his stricken muscles. He continued to sweep the big pick back and forth across the autoharp strings, changing chords at will, lost in music he was creating nearly effortlessly.

"Do you sing?" I asked when he took a break to rest his hands.

"Yeah, I can sing a little."

I slid one of the music books across the table in front of us. "Autoharp is a great accompaniment for singing." I paged to "Oh, Susannah," since it conveniently used only three chords and I had never met anyone who didn't know this folk song. He caught on quickly when I explained how to interpret the book's markings.

After I did a short demo for him, singing and playing together, he said he would try it at home. Was he getting weary or was he afraid MS had robbed him of his singing voice, another one of its sneaky ravages to the body. "Singing is only an afterthought. Remember this is just for you. No right or wrong."

"This music is making me feel so dreamy, sleepy."

"The strings not only vibrate separately but they cause each other to vibrate. That's the intense feeling you're having; the vibrations affect every atom of your body."

"I'm going to sleep like a baby tonight."

He and Jenny looked at each other. She raised her eyebrows, then turned toward the wall where our clock was rhythmically ticking. "It's been a long workweek for us, we better get going," she said helping Kevin pull his chair out from the dining room table to stand up. She handed him his cane and Gordon walked ahead of them into the hallway to get their coats. I gathered up the autoharp, music book, and pick, and placed it all in the autoharp case, clicking the three clasps into place, then carried it to the hallway where Kevin and Jenny were slipping into their coats.

"Thank you so much. We really felt at home. Dessert, a nice fire and my autoharp lesson. This was great."

"I think this will really be good for Kevin," Jenny said as I handed her the autoharp.

"If anything sounds off to you, a string or two might be out of tune. I can easily fix that for you," I said as they stepped toward the front door. I was unsure how sensitive Kevin might be to an overly sharp or flat note. I myself cringed at out of tune instruments and voices, and I wanted to protect Kevin from any disturbing sounds. "Let me know how it goes if you want to," I added as they walked out the door.

"Good luck with the wedding plans," Gordon called out to them as they walked down the sidewalk toward the driveway.

"I think everything's taken care of," Jenny said turning around.

"Good night," I said as they approached their car.

Kevin's low, snazzy sports car was not parked in the driveway. Instead a sensible, four door white sedan awaited. I saw Jenny open the back door and set the autoharp on the backseat, before she opened the driver's door and slid in. Kevin took his time to walk around to the passenger seat, opened the door and got in using his cane for balance. Perhaps, night driving was difficult for him. Or maybe he was extra fatigued by this time of night.

Whatever the reason, this duo had it figured out. As Jenny said, "Things were taken care of."

Chapter 17

Out of Tune

I got it wrong.

A year later Kevin and I met for lunch as we had agreed to do. I had emailed him and asked to meet. I was shocked when I saw him. He was terribly thin, his wrinkled clothes hung on him, his hair was disheveled. And he had driven up in a different car, not a low-lying snazzy sports car, but a small dirty black Toyota sedan.

We didn't meet at Luella's. He said he was tired of that place so we joined up at Homegrown, a local healthy food place where every representation of the Asheville community dined side by side on local produce and responsibly farmed meats, fish, and poultry. I had recently discovered their noteworthy fried chicken.

After we ordered lunch we found a table for two and he began his story. I was saddened to see that his gait was more jerky and he trembled more noticeably.

"I'm glad you called. I've been a mess. Drinking like a fool, eating badly. Even smoking; and more than cigarettes. I've wrecked two cars." He could see the curiosity, the concern cross my face.

He continued. "Jenny left me six months after our wedding. She took off with another guy. I didn't even know where she was until recently when her lawyer contacted me. She wants a divorce."

This time he could see shock in my expression. I held my breath, closed my eyes to avoid his, then exhaled as I brought my head down.

"Yeah. It hit me so hard. I've been struggling with depression; even thought about suicide a few times. I'm in counseling and on some drugs now and I think I'm starting to come around. I needed your call."

I didn't know how to respond so I just said I was sorry this had happened to him. Then I added, "I'm shocked." There was silence until he spoke.

"Remember when you told me I ought to write my story? You're a writer and I want to pick your brain."

He elaborated how he had been sitting at his computer in front of a blank page, not knowing where to start. He asked about the classes I took, the people I knew. How I began my writing. Our conversation continued through lunch.

Once he had assimilated my comments about writing and possible approaches, he added more about his life.

"Since I still live in Jenny's and my house and she isn't coming back, I'm in the process of turning it into an Airbnb. I need the money to buy her out and having regular guests come and go will lift my spirits."

My worry dissipated as he described what he had done to ready the house to receive company. He showed me photos of his beautifully decorated, polished home. I noticed the gleaming wooden floors, a guitar leaning against a bookcase, bright artwork on the walls, and the garden he kept in his backyard.

"A veggie garden?"

"Yeah. I really want to eat healthy again. My neighbors are so good to me. They built the raised beds, hauled in the soil, so I can reach the plants more easily, and last fall they raked my whole yard."

As he told me more, I relaxed, knowing he really was going to be fine. He talked about his network of friends and his family who supported him despite his fierce desire for total independence. He was still working at Nantahala and even dated once in a while. He laughed when he told me his doctor had given him a prescription for Viagra. "I don't need it." Then he added that he had filled it just in case.

I wondered what role I played in his life, especially after his Viagra comment—friend, confessor, wise woman, writer, counselor, musician? I was glad he felt he could talk freely to me. Perhaps, his openness kept him going. He was not in denial, sick with secrets.

We parted with a hug and a promise to get together. My head still spun with the shock of Jenny's quick departure and Kevin's dark descent. She and Kevin seemed so mature, secure in their relationship. Although I felt bad for Kevin, I understood how Jenny, after realizing the gravity of her commitment to Kevin, may have done the only thing she knew to do—run away. I wondered if she felt guilty.

Kevin and I continue to meet for lunch once a year to catch up and stay in touch. He is writing his story and planning on taking some classes. His Airbnb is always full and he is delighted with his guests, many from other countries. His garden is thriving and he is eating well.

However, his disease is destroying his body. He can no longer drive and he relies on a walker to help him drag his legs one at a time to walk.

After our most recent lunch I offered to drive him back to his workplace. He accepted the ride and even allowed me to load his walker in my trunk.

"Yeah. My body isn't doing great, but I'm happy anyway."

After I dropped him off at his office, I got in my car and cried all the way home.

Chapter 18

Sit Still

Sit still." Those words were what I heard as I sat plastered to the front row of the polished mahogany church pew, my little brother Glenn seated beside me. My legs dangled and my bare thighs squeaked against the shiny wood if I wiggled. My dress, one my Grandma Lewis paid for at the fancy-dancy Jane Shalfont Dress Shoppe in West Chester, Pennsylvania, was one I actually liked; a burgundy red, with long sleeves, a slightly flouncy skirt, and very few ruffles.

Glenn's short, five-year-old's legs stuck straight out from the pew. I, at nine, was his keeper in that echoey, high-ceilinged stone church, much more grand than our family church. My mother was a paid soprano soloist in the afternoon Christmas concert of Handel's *Messiah*. My father must've been singing baritone in the choir because he did not sit with Glenn and me.

I expected our placement in the front row provided an eagle's eye view of our behavior from my parents' positions in the raised choir loft. I think the choir wore black robes; but my mother donned a pure white robe and was seated ahead of the choir, out front, with the other soloists. She looked like an angel. The small orchestra was placed just below the choir loft, very close to me and my brother.

My father had handed me a program with the libretto written out so I could follow along. Glenn was not a reader yet, though later, when he could read, he became quite the bookworm, unlike me. I was a doer more than a reader. My mother valued readers.

The folded *Messiah* handout was not all that wordy, so I reasoned Glenn and I could sit still for an hour or so and then enjoy the promised holiday goodies at the reception afterwards in the fellowship hall.

The conductor raised his baton and the orchestra began the instrumental introduction called "Sinfonia." I pointed at the word in the bulletin so Glenn could see where we were. As a violin student and a member of an orchestra myself, the proximity of the violinists with their scores, like menus, spread across their music stands, captured my eyes; I tried to follow their notes, listen to how their parts flew in and around the other instruments, like a call-and-answer song I learned in youth choir.

A tall, lanky male soloist stood, then sang. "Comfort, ye." My attention was drawn to his rich, fluid voice. Then he sang again. "Comfort ye, my people." I looked down at my hand out. Wait a minute. He already sang that line. He sang it again and again. I wondered what was up, but I sat still as instructed.

"Saith your God. Saith your God." He did it again. Why does this man need to repeat himself?

The afternoon of *The Messiah* proceeded just like that, repeating the words over and over. I didn't wear a watch in those days but I knew a lot of time had passed and that I had to shift my position on the pew. I waited until the chorus was singing and the orchestra playing to wiggle around and move my bare legs, now stuck to the pew. I hoped no one heard them squeak their own high-pitched music. Glenn was able to squirm since his legs were fully covered by his dress slacks; eventually he even laid his head on my lap, stretched out long in the pew and fell asleep. I hoped this was okay with my parents. I remained upright and still, like a little soldier.

Then my mother rose from her seat, her white robe shimmering, her blond hair shining in the spotlights, her blue eyes sparkling. She raised her score and awaited the end of the orchestra's introduction, then sang, "And he shall feed his flock, like a shepherd." Her clear, high soprano rang out over the crowded sanctuary. I was so proud of her I sat even taller. But, she sang her words over and over again just like the chorus and the other soloists before her. I became impatient, wanted her to get over her solo, wanted this marathon to end. Glenn rolled over on my lap while she sang. I wondered if he recognized her voice. We were used to her rehearsing regularly at home, accompanying herself on the piano in the living room.

Finally, the orchestra launched into a lively introduction to the last words on my hand-out. Everyone, including the audience, stood. My parents had told me about rising, like the Queen of England did, for the "Hallelujah Chorus," but I could not comply because Glenn's head was resting on my lap, weighing me down. So I sat there, worried that they thought I was disobeying musical etiquette, disrespecting royalty.

I'll never know if I truly felt the joy, the energy of the music of the famous "Hallelujah Chorus" with its high, soaring Baroque trumpets and heavy rhythmic timpani, or if my exuberance that afternoon stemmed from relief that *The Messiah* was finally over and I could move around, get to the desserts downstairs. The applause was long and loud enough to awaken Glenn, who sat up wide-eyed and pink-faced with wrinkle imprints from my cranberry dress's skirt etched in his cheeks.

My mother was surrounded by well-wishers congratulating her on her performance. Again I had to sit still with Glenn and await my parents' accompaniment to the tables of goodies served down below. When we finally descended the steep stone steps, long lines of reception-goers blocked my view of the cookies. By time we inched our way to the reception tables, my heart sank seeing that the plates of cookies had thinned out. I had looked forward to the treats all afternoon. At last, my father's hand reached into the middle of a table and picked up two chocolate chip cookies, his and my favorites; he gave me both of them and then reached in and got two more for himself. My musical torture was rewarded, as promised. Mom handed Glenn two peanut butter cookies, their favorites. I doubt if she ate anything; she was always concerned about her figure, as she called it.

From Thanksgiving to Christmas our household buzzed with preparation, mostly my mother's frenzied planning and rehearsing. In addition to her paid solo jobs, she hosted a holiday piano recital for her private students and their families, directed the adult choirs, and prepared special concerts of church music for the holidays. Leading up to these events her calendar was solid with dates, and her mood soured with each approaching event. Somehow she added decorating the house, baking and frosting Christmas cookies, sewing matching holiday attire for all of us (this was a fiasco since she was not a good seamstress and her frustration added to her mounting bad mood). I recall the homemade red plaid vests we wore one year for the family photo that Dad took with his fancy camera mounted on a tripod with the timer set so he could hustle to his spot on the sofa with the rest of us. Once he developed the photos Mom wrote and mimeographed the annual family Christmas letter, then addressed and mailed them to a long list of friends and relatives.

Meanwhile, her fatigue and her stress often landed her in bed with a cold, laryngitis, a bad cough; enemy maladies for anyone, but especially for a singer. She slathered her throat and chest with Vicks and tied one of my father's hankies around her neck to protect her clothing. She sucked on foul-smelling throat lozenges, and several times a day she bent over a pan of boiling water steeped with menthol crystals, inhaling the medicated steam. I knew when she had to "breathe crystals," as she called it, that things were not going to go well in the household. When she went to bed I was handed the role of mother, cook, house manager.

Our break-neck Christmas Eve began with a list of hers and our duties by the hour. At 4:30 all of us were seated in the dining room eating bowls of her version of goulash over rice, a dish she prepared in the morning and let simmer in the electric fry pan all day. This, with a last-minute green vegetable, was our dinner. Cookies and ice cream usually came in between the first and second service at church, when she rushed home to help my father put the younger kids to bed and watch them hang their Christmas stockings before she swept out the door for the next service.

I had musical parts alongside my mother in both early services, so when I read my list, I saw that I had to bathe, fix my hair, and wear my Christmas dress, covered with an apron, to the dinner table before my violin and I were loaded in the station wagon to drive to church.

My Grandmother Lewis always attended one of the early services so she could hear me and my mother perform. She visited every Christmas but was not keen on babysitting unless my brothers were asleep, so I took on the babysitting role after my musical appearances, allowing my dad to drive to church and sing in Mom's choir at the candlelight service at eleven. When Grandma visited, I dreaded sharing my room with her; she snored and her floral scented body powder made my eyes water. She got my bed and I had to sleep on a narrow, rickety military cot in a hot, tight sleeping bag. I was easily overstimulated and had difficulty falling asleep on normal nights, so the church services, the excitement of Christmas, and the upheaval in my bedroom, usually kept me wide-eyed all night. I was exhausted like my mother but no one noticed. That's when I usually succumbed to a sore throat, a cold and an ear infection.

I have never been one to sit still. Like my parents, I filled my calendar with activities, and was expected to do so. I've learned through difficult experiences that staying busy every moment is harmful to me. I get sick. Or resentful. Or suffer from insomnia, emotional overload. Blessed with an active, creative brain and a natural outgoing drive, I move through life with curiosity, wide open to people, places, things and the next project.

I am hypersensitive, a person who does not easily filter out incoming sensory data. Just months ago a friend called about a new book she had read, *The Empath's Survival Guide* by Dr. Judith Orloff. "You've got to read this," she said over the phone. On occasion I have been asked if I was an empath, but I never really knew what that meant and shrugged it off.

My jaw dropped as I found my story in this book. Now I understood why, when I hear or perform music, it stays with me for several days; why I absorb peoples' emotions, body language; why I become anxious in loud, confusing settings, and nauseated when food odor from all-day cooking permeates the house. Like many empaths, I need darkness, quiet and an exact temperature to sleep, and total quiet to read or study. Often I compose, memorize, mull, rewrite, re-live in never-ending loops, day or night. I startle easily. I do not travel well. The sensory overload I experience causes me to tense my body into fight or flight mode, leading to debilitating muscle spasms in my neck, shoulders, and back. Often the spasms have me tight with pain before I recognize what's hit me. Swimming, massage, walking, yoga, spiritual practice, and meditation are not luxuries but necessities for me. When I do not sing, hear or play music I feel a void.

On several occasions I have known in advance that someone has died or become very ill when I had no reason to expect this outcome.

Orloff estimates that 20% of the population are empaths in varying degrees, persons whose brains cannot block or filter out incoming sensual data. Studies have not yet figured out why this is so. I asked Gordon to read the book. His jaw dropped, too. "You are really an empath, and not just a lightweight one." This new knowledge, another unsolicited opportunity to understand myself, has taken me a step further to actually love who I am, feel okay about my quirks, my requirements for and difficulties with navigating this life.

And I am extroverted, which is not a healthy pairing with hypersensitivity, being an empath. When I need to retreat, to rest, and to tend myself with loving kindness, my urge to get out there, take care of others, be the leader, join the fray—the traits more valued by this world and by my family of origin—override and silence my utter physical, emotional, psychological, and spiritual exhaustion. Extroversion has taken the lead in my life. I have mistaken the attention and admiration for being a performer as genuine love. I've nearly killed myself in its pursuit. This pattern began in childhood, encouraged and rewarded, and its hard lesson repeats itself as I learn to pay attention to myself. To sit still.

But the pairing of empath and extrovert also has its benefits. As an artist, my absorption of and memory for details infuse my writing and my music with depth, connection, beauty. My sensitivity to others allows me to easily interact with nearly every person I meet. This gift carries over to performances, presentations, therapeutic music sessions where I try to make eye contact with every person in my presence. I want people I meet to feel welcome, included, worthy, loved.

And I think this is why I can ask strangers to eat lunch with me.

During a recent holiday season, I became quite ill, a result of pushing my limits, thinking I could tackle extra music performances, writing deadlines, parties, and volunteer activities. The usual family Christmas preparations were easy, now that it was only Gordon and me. Just one more thing here and there wouldn't hurt, I reasoned.

I especially overdid it on an early December Saturday when I ignored my gut feelings: I set up, appeared, and performed at two book fairs in one day, running from one to the other to keep up. I never sat still. I was cold in one venue, hot in another; and I shook many hands that day, talked to the browsing crowds, played music for them, and generally behaved like the old Robin, the one who saw her mother demonstrate what a woman could do if she put her mind and her energies to it.

After packing up in the late afternoon from both book fairs, I came home exhausted, but I squeezed in a sitting meditation between dinner and the time we needed to leave for a choral concert. Meditation and the prospect of hearing music were the only magic I thought I needed to get out the door again.

By Tuesday I was bleary-eyed, achy, feverish, congested, and coughing furiously. I managed to get to the doctor before eleven inches of snow, forecast as flurries, surprised us in western North Carolina and shut down roads and stores. The verdict: pneumonia, bronchitis, and a sinus infection. I came home from the doctor and collapsed.

By Thursday, the night of the annual *Messiah* singalong, the roads were clear, but I was still hazy and droopy. For years I had enjoyed this event; I would tote my own score, all penciled up with markings from past performances, and sit in the alto section of the crowded church. This year, instead of adding my voice to the Asheville Symphony and Chorus, plus reveling in the gorgeous professional soloists, I would be staying home, wrapped in fleece blankets, taking antibiotics and Tylenol, slugging down hot tea, huffing on an inhaler. Gordon would go without me.

The morning after the singalong, feeling slightly better, I opened up my score which still sat on the kitchen table, located my *Messiah* CD among a tall stash of holiday music, and placed it in the CD player and sat down. The "Sinfonia" filled the breakfast room as winter sun poured in the bay window by the table. My singing voice was silenced by my illness, but the Atlanta Symphony with the Robert Shaw Chorale substituted for me. The tenor's solo voice sang out above the orchestra. "Comfort ye; comfort ye, my people." I settled back in my chair, warmed, comforted. And still. The music broke through my congestion, my headache and fever.

And then it happened. The soprano soloist, as if singing from a heavenly place, lifted her clear perfect voice above the orchestra and began: "And he shall feed his flock, like a shepherd." I was transfixed; the light intensified. I held my breath, and looked up. My mother appeared in front of me in the light wearing a shimmering gown; her hair was now gray, but her blue eyes still shone and her voice captured me with its magnificence. At that moment I knew in a profound way, this was what she had lived for: to sing these classical solos, share her talent, her expertise. This was where she was meant to be. This was the woman she wanted to be.

"Robin, I had offers to sing on the radio," she told me a number of times, her eyes looking out and far away. As a senior voice major in college she had been the overwhelming choice by the music department to sing the coveted "O, Holy Night" solo in the formal, candlelight Christmas Concert held annually in the massive, spired limestone church on campus. Her choices for marriage and family snuffed out her dream. She had gotten lost in four children, my father, housework, piano lessons and church music. But her heart beat to sing as a soloist.

"And he shall feed his flock like a shepherd. And he shall gather the lambs with his arms. And carry them in his bosom." I wondered what those words meant to her. Or how the music moved her.

She should have never been a mother, I thought. She should've been a full-time professional singer. She had been unable to feed me, gather me, or carry me in her bosom, what I had yearned for all my life. Her insensitivity to me had compounded my struggles to identify, accept and manage my empathic, extroverted self.

With my throat choked up, I swallowed hard as the soprano's voice filled the room. My mother didn't realize her dreams, step into her true self, follow her right path. The expectations of her own mother and of the 1940s distracted her, derailed her. Now I knew why her roles as mother and wife were executed with a sense of duty rather than a sense of love. Her love was elsewhere. I had felt her resentment, and let her passive aggressive demands on me define our relationship. Maybe I was supposed to fulfill her dreams. But she didn't respect my style of music making, I didn't measure up.

But, sitting there in the sunlight, my tears also fell because I had not allowed myself to penetrate my hard layer of disdain for her. I had not respected or appreciated her music-making. I had hardly ever complimented her singing or piano-playing. I derided her for her reliance on printed music. As an adult, I smirked to myself when she played or sang in public, inwardly criticized her, smugly told myself I was the better musician. Even up to her final breath, as I stood over her chanting, comforting her using my skills as a therapeutic musician, I didn't know whether my music reached her, or if it suited her.

Now, in my kitchen, as my mother sang her glorious solo, I wept for both of us: our conflicts, our standoffs, our competition, our overdoing. Our losses. I felt my throat burn, my chest expand. I yearned for the openness we never had over lunch together.

Sitting still, turning my head slowly, staring out the window at the white winter landscape, I forgave her.

Then I forgave myself.

Chapter 19

A Table in the Corner

I decided to go it alone.

Gordon and I were in New York City celebrating his milestone birthday with two of our children who flew in for the occasion and wined and dined us in splendor; after their departure we had part of a free day before our Road Scholar opera week began. Opera was more for him than me, his recent discovery of it prompting our trip.

New York City's environment is not kind to me. After only three days my nervous system was already wound tightly. And we would be there for five more days. Smells of street foods mingled with rancid garbage odors; screams of ambulances, fire trucks, police cars pierced the atmosphere round the clock; an overload of people, stores, advertisements flashed one after the other, and the constant bumping and jostling on the streets and the subway kept me feeling unsafe. It was all coming at me, into me faster than I could discharge it. Despite retreating to our fairly quiet hotel room for a hot shower, a breathing meditation, some reading and writing, or a session of yoga, my empathic self wouldn't settle down. I yearned for a swim or a massage.

And I realized that our hotel room could be a refuge only if I had it to myself. Of course, Gordon and I were sharing it and we had been together every minute since we arrived in the City. I was extra-tuned-in to him as well.

Even after a decent night's sleep I had awakened that morning feeling grumpy, achy, nauseated, resentful, and near tears, signs that I needed to tend myself.

"I want to go back to the Metropolitan Museum of Art today," Gordon announced. I could feel my whole body stiffen. I heard my inner voice say I ought to go since likely this would be my last trip to the City, and on our special tour with a docent the day before we had seen only some highlights of the huge collection. I took several deep breaths and was able to hear my authentic voice say out loud, "I really need some me time, some time to just kick around." I felt myself melt.

Gordon and I are used to doing our own things. I may have even heard some relief in his voice when he replied that going alone would be great. He assembled his subway map, his hat, and water bottle into his backpack, kissed me good-bye and left our room.

Years ago Julia Cameron's workbook *The Artist's Way* introduced me to the idea of taking an "artist's date" as she called it. I have come to call it "wandering" and my version usually entails being alone possibly gardening, walking, shopping, sitting on my deck listening to birds, playing or listening to music, driving on a back road, maybe even asking strangers to eat with me, listening to their stories. But I am the one who chooses what direction I take, and there is really no agenda. I'm open. Over the years I have rescued myself, discharged emotional or sensory overload, filled emptiness, discovered new ideas, found inspiration, enjoyed the "holy mystery" of God in these "dates." Cameron is right that creatives need time to let their artistic juices relax, bump into ideas, enjoy, play, experiment. And for me, during these dates I take time to get into myself, detach from over-sensing others and my environment, which ironically takes me out of myself.

I sat down on the bed and decided what I wanted to do. I thought a short walk to Designer Shoe Warehouse and then maybe Macy's on 34th St. sounded easy, familiar, even exciting. I didn't need a thing at either of the stores, the best part. Pure wandering.

The four floors of DSW connected by mostly nonworking escalators, was populated by more non-English- than English-speaking patrons. I played a game with myself guessing what languages I heard, a form of music to my ears. Parades of sample shoes lined the tops of the display cases while stacks of boxed shoes were tucked below, their sizes and descriptions turned toward the aisle. My attention was immediately drawn in. This really was New York City. Relaxing? Maybe not, but distracting, for sure.

Seeing all the shoes led me to fixate on the idea of finding a pair of casual black slip-ons. Who knew where this came from? I concentrated, even obsessed over finding these shoes and tried on at least thirty pairs in this style with no luck. It didn't matter. I worked my way through the last aisle stepping around customers surrounded by towers of boxes, pools of shoes; men and women hunched over their feet tying laces, slipping on yet another trial shoe or standing sideways in front of a mirror evaluating a shoe's fit and style.

I felt my nausea again along with some light-headedness and started to leave to find some lunch when I spotted the perfect shoe. What I needed more was food, a chair and some quiet, but I overrode my needs when I saw that this shoe was right there in my size, a miracle of sorts since I wear a women' s size eleven. I slid out that last box of shoes from the shelving, tried them on. Perfect shoes. Perfect fit. There is joy in such findings, and I smiled to feel it, a sign that fight or flight was itself fleeing.

I dug into my purse to find some ginger-and-chamomile cubes

to suck on, a suggestion my herbalist friend had given me when she learned how strongly I reacted to stimuli. As I stood in line to pay and then walked down the broken escalator steps, I felt the cubes go to work on my nerves and my stomach.

Macy's was equally crowded; a weekend sale sucked customers in through the glass revolving doors, smudged by so many handprints. Dizzied by the glittering displays, the mixed scents of expensive perfumes and lotions, the hustling and nudging of people in a hurry and the heavy screaming rock music on the first floor, I was unsure if I could stay in this atmosphere. After finding a kiosk with information about the numerous floors, I rode several escalators to the women's department. With each ascent, the sound level decreased.

The women's department was carpeted, fairly low-ceilinged and the music was nearly indecipherable. I joined other women quietly pawing through the sale racks. Most of them, like me, were alone. Perhaps this solo exercise of shopping by themselves, wandering through racks of clothing and accessories, was as calming to them as it was to me today. As I combed the department looking for nothing, but imagining myself in various outfits, many of them odd and outlandish, I felt another wave of joy lighten my day, but it was time to leave and seek food. As I left my eyes landed on a gray long-sleeve tee for $3 and some charcoal exercise capris for $10, both in my size. I didn't need them, but I could use them. I felt another victory smile ripple across my face as I handed the cashier my credit card.

I knew lunch would probably be my final stop on my artist date, but where would I eat in this maze? After the exquisite meals with our kids, I wanted something light and healthy.

When I finally found an old working wooden down escalator, I stepped aboard. I noticed a sign for several eateries, including a restaurant called

Salad Bowl on the fourth floor. I experienced another moment of joy, another perfect fit when I saw the tiny, tucked-away restaurant space and read the menu for made-to-order salads. Like the capris and tee and the perfect black shoes, this find was another source of satisfaction, and even a bargain for NYC. I ordered mixed greens, then chose from a colorful, plenteous assortment of additional ingredients, some recognizable, some foreign. I felt adventurous and didn't even ask the salad maker any questions as I pointed to the add-ons I wanted for my salad.

With a full bowl I scanned the dining area and saw a couple of possible single diners with whom to share lunch. I stopped myself, paid attention and realized I wanted to be alone. There was no "something" urging me to ask a stranger to eat with me. My extroverted voice was silenced. My empath voice sat me down at a table in the corner by myself.

I didn't need the company, the distraction, the input, the connection, the affirmation to feel whole, worthy, loved. I could do that for myself now. I placed my tray on the table and sat down. Lunch turned into a meditation. Before I took a bite I sat still, then silently blessed my food and the young salad makers behind the counter who had prepared the large brimming salad bowl in front of me. My mind stayed in the moment, in this time of listening to myself, this time of self-care.

A young Indian couple with a toddler and a baby, beautiful little girls with thick, dark, curly eyelashes and sly smiles, took the table next to me. Their presence provided me an easy opportunity to engage with them. But I only acknowledged them with a gentle nod, and returned to my own lunch, my reverie.

When my salad bowl was empty, I rose to bus my dishes to the bins near the exit. But before I departed, I walked over to the salad counter to thank the young staff for my meal, a gesture I had begun to practice.

"Thank you for a delicious lunch," I said. They looked up from their tasks, taken aback by my comment. I enjoyed how their solemn faces lit up with simple words of gratitude; after delivering my used bowl, I walked out of the salad nook.

How curious, possibly coincidental that in the midst of New York City I found solitude in a bustling shoe store, a crowded department store and a quiet salad restaurant. My emptiness was filled by so many choices. My life tasted good: many flavors, alone and together. A harmonious mix.

I felt lucky to be open for lunch.

About the Author

Robin Russell Gaiser earned her B.A. in English at The College of William and Mary, where she also sang and played with a folk-rock group, both on campus and in venues in Richmond, Virginia, and Washington, D.C. After graduation she taught writing and literature in Fairfax County, Virginia; then, while raising her family, she gave private lessons in guitar and dulcimer and performed publicly under the auspices of the Fairfax County Council of the Arts and the Arlington Humanities Program. She also sang in classical choirs and joined The Mill Run Dulcimer Band, recording seven albums now included in the Smithsonian collection.

With her children grown, Robin earned an MA in psychology from Marymount University and worked as a high school guidance counselor for eight years. Then, after relocating to upstate New York and becoming caregiver—and bedside musician—for her dying father, she enrolled in a certification program for therapeutic musicians. As a Certified Music Practitioner (CMP), she is trained to provide live, bedside, one-on-one acoustic music to critically and chronically ill, elderly, and dying patients.

After forty-three years in northern Virginia and eight years in upstate New York, Robin and her husband relocated to Asheville, NC, where she has pursued both her music and her writing. Her nonfiction has appeared in the women's literary journal *Minerva Rising* ("Angels," Dec. 2012) in three anthologies of short stories published by Grateful Steps Publishing: *Drowning Allison & other stories* ("Yellow," 2012), *The Cricket & other stories* ("Doorways," 2014), and *Bits of Sugar & other stories* ("I'll Fly Away," 2016); and in *Writing in Circles: A Celebration of Women's Writing*, published by Sunburst Cabin Press ("Took Out the Tattered," 2014). Her essay "How Music Led Me to Memoir" appeared on the blog, Memoir Writers' Journey, published by Kathy Pooler, in 2014. Robin was a guest columnist for the *Great Smokies Review* spring, 2018 issue with her piece, "Take Note."

Musical Morphine: Transforming Pain One Note at a Time (Pisgah Press; June, 2016), Robin's first book, a memoir, was named a finalist in the Best American Book Awards for 2017. Robin was chosen to give a TEDx Talk titled "Good Vibrations: Less Drugs, More Music" on March 3, 2018, at UNCA. This talk is available for viewing on Robin's website and on You Tube.

Robin volunteers as a musician for homeless shelters, homebound seniors, aphasia patients, and for nonprofit fundraisers. Besides her reputation as a musician and author, she is known as a gifted speaker, presenter and performer. She and her husband are the parents of one daughter and two sons, and grandparents of three.

She may be contacted via her website, www.robingaiser.com or by email at robingaiser@gmail.com.

Acknowledgments

Thanks always to my editor/publisher Andy Reed at Pisgah Press whose careful reading and belief in my writing encourages me onward; and to Elizabeth Luytens, my instructor who teaches classes of serious writers and critiquers in Master Prose through the Great Smokies Writing Program at UNCA. Thanks to the many writers in her classes whose astute comments and suggestions helped me get to the real meat of *Open for Lunch* over four semesters of hard work together.

Thanks to Laurie McCarriar for cover design, bio photo, web design, and social media management.

Thanks to my longtime friend Carol Even for her suggestion of *Open for Lunch* as my book title.

Special thanks to all those who trusted me enough to accept an invitation to eat lunch together as perfect strangers. I am also gratified that some of those lunch mates remain in my life as friends.

Also available from Pisgah Press

Barry Burgess

Mombie: The Zombie Mom	$16.95

Donna Lisle Burton

Letting Go: Collected Poems 1983-2003	$14.95
Way Past Time for Reflecting	$17.95

Michael Amos Cody

Gabriel's Songbook	$17.95

Robin Russell Gaiser

Musical Morphine: Transforming Pain One Note at a Time	$17.95

Finalist, USA Book Awards for Health: Alternative Medicine, 2017

Chris Highland

A Freethinker's Gospel: Essays for a Sacred, Secular World	$16.95

C. Robert Jones

I Like It Here! Adventures in the Wild & Wonderful World of Theatre	$30.00
Lanky Tales, Vol. I: The Bird Man & other stories	$9.00
Lanky Tales, Vol. II: Billy Red Wing & other stories	$9.00
Lanky Tales, Vol. III: A Good and Faithful Friend & other stories	$9.00
The Mystery at Claggett Cove	$9.00

Jeff Douglas Messer

Red-state, White-guy Blues	$15.95

A. D. Reed

Reed's Homophones: a comprehensive book of sound-alike words	$14.95

2018 sponsor of NPR's *Says You!*

Dave Richards

Swords in their Hands: George Washington and the Newburgh Conspiracy	$24.95

Finalist, USA Book Award for History, 2014

Sarah-Ann Smith

Trang Sen: A Novel of Vietnam	$19.50

Nan Socolow

Invasive Procedures: Earthquakes, Calamities, & poems from the midst of life	$17.95

RF Wilson

THE RICK RYDER MYSTERY SERIES

Deadly Dancing		$15.95
Killer Weed		$14.95
The Pot Professor	available Winter 2019	$15.95

Pisgah Press, LLC
PO Box 9663, Asheville, NC 28815-0663
www.pisgahpress.com

CPSIA information can be obtained
at www.ICGtesting.com
Printed in the USA
BVHW071401091219
566081BV00021B/1986/P